Praise ...

Don't Die before You're Dead

I met Joy Blessing when I was a junior airline pilot. Joy was a flight attendant. Before the flight, I had seen her name on the paper work and thought to myself, *Joy Blessing, there has to be a story there.* Was there ever a story! Her book is yet another amazing part of the story of Joy Blessing. It's an amazing testimony of the trials and tribulations, being tested yet living a fully dedicated life of faith, and even through the tough times remaining Joy-Full! Her journey through life, and 39 minutes of death, and life again has given Joy a miraculous and amazing testimony that will bless you.

—Tim Heibel, Airline Captain —Fellow Sojourner

***

What a wonderful insight into the power of prayer and believing in the Bible! What Joy experienced on that day should open up one's eyes to the Glory of God. The power of believing that if you follow the word of God on this earth, when you are called home, your soul will be welcomed in Heaven. This world is definitely a constant battle of evil (the devil) and good.

—Claire Croskey, Retired Emergency Medical Technician—A True Believer and Faithful Friend

***

In this this death to life true story, God manifests His power to heal and restore the human body. The narrative is about a woman who died and was brought back to life in unusual circumstances. This piece magnifies God's grace and mercy of the miraculous. It shows us that the Lord has a destiny for each one of our lives. The epic is extraordinarily well written. If you want an inspiring and thrilling saga of despair to victory, this book will move you to expect hope.

—**Karen Hembrough**, Medical Missionary to Guatemala

***

Joy's poignant journey of her health crisis draws readers to understand the correlation between faith and medical technology. Her prognosis of a future with limited physical opportunities was turned upside down – and today Joy now leads a life of limitless potential of joy and inspiration.

—**Rev. Glynn Ferguson**, Owner of Sensational Ceremonies

DON'T DIE before YOU'RE DEAD

LIVING with a HEART OF JOY

JOY BLESSING

DEAD FOR 39 MINUTES

Published by KHARIS PUBLISHING, an imprint of KHARIS MEDIA LLC.

Copyright © 2024 Joy Blessing

ISBN-13: 978-1-63746-248-5

ISBN-10: 1-63746-248-4

Library of Congress Control Number: 2024931132

Unless otherwise indicated, Scripture quotations are taken from *The Living Bible*, copyright © 1971 by Tyndale House Foundation. Used by permission of Tyndale House Foundation, Carol Stream, Illinois 60188. All rights reserved.

AMP: Scripture taken from the AMPLIFIED® BIBLE, Copyright © 1954, 1958, 1962, 1964, 1965, 1987 by the Lockman Foundation Used by Permission. (www.Lockman.org)

NIV: Scripture taken from THE HOLY BIBLE, NEW INTERNATIONAL VERSION ®. Copyright© 1973, 1978, 1984, 2011 by Biblica, Inc.™. Used by permission of Zondervan.

KJV: Scriptures marked KJV are taken from the KING JAMES VERSION, public domain.

NKJV: Scriptures marked NKJV are taken from the NEW KING JAMES VERSION ®. Copyright© 1982 by Thomas Nelson, Inc. Used by permission. All rights reserved.

NLT: *New Living Translation.* Copyright© 1996, 2004, 2007, by Tyndale House Foundation. Used by permission of Tyndale House Publishers, Inc. Carol Stream, IL 60188. All rights reserved.

NLV: Scripture quotations marked NLV are taken from the *New Life Version*, copyright © 1969 and 2003. Used by permission of Barbour Publishing, Inc., Uhrichsville, Ohio 44683. All rights reserved.

All KHARIS PUBLISHING products are available at special quantity discounts for bulk purchase for sales promotions, premiums, fund-raising, and educational needs. For details, contact:

Kharis Media LLC

Tel: 1-630-909-3405

support@kharispublishing.com

www.kharispublishing.com

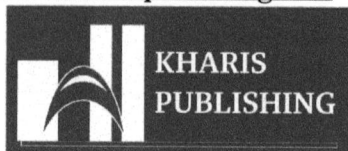

KHARIS
PUBLISHING

DON'T DIE before YOU'RE DEAD

LIVING with a HEART OF JOY

JOY BLESSING

DEAD FOR 39 MINUTES

Published by KHARIS PUBLISHING, an imprint of KHARIS
MEDIA LLC.
Copyright © 2024 Joy Blessing
ISBN-13: 978-1-63746-248-5
ISBN-10: 1-63746-248-4
Library of Congress Control Number: 2024931132
All KHARIS PUBLISHING products are available at special quantity
discounts for bulk purchase for sales promotions, premiums, fund-raising,
and educational needs. For details, contact:
Kharis Media LLC
Tel: 1-630-909-3405
support@kharispublishing.com
www.kharispublishing.com

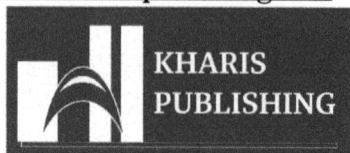

KHARIS
PUBLISHING

FOREWORD

Are you *alive*? … *Truly* living?

Or are you just *existing?* Technically your heart is still beating, but you are not living with *all* your *heart*. The passion of a joyful life is missing from most days – maybe *all* of them.

Perhaps you're in your senior years and feel as if the best of life is behind you, or that you're no longer needed or wanted, or that you are *too old* to do what you love most.

But you could even be in the *prime* of life and yet just "going through the motions" of existence – eating, drinking, working, sleeping, etc., with little genuine delight or purpose.

Maybe you're just too discouraged, frustrated, tired, weary, anxious, and overwhelmed with taking care of the cares of this world, your family and even strangers, when not really taking care of yourself.

If you have been hurt *too* much, sick *too* much, rejected *too* much, failed *too* much, it can sometimes seem that it is just *too* hard to even *try* to live with any *real* joy.

Perhaps you are overwhelmed by perpetual "doomsday" warnings in a world that seems to have gone crazy. You cope with an attitude of "whatever happens, happens."

Maybe you think, *I'm fine, you're fine, everything is fine.*

Are your days filled with the same old things and no expectations of anything better?

Or maybe you are just stuck. You want to live life to the fullest, but just don't know how or lack the resources to do so, or you feel inadequate or helpless to help yourself.

Do you sometimes feel paralyzed in moving forward to find a way where there seems to be *no* way?

What does it matter anyway? We are bombarded with this matters, that matters, those matter, but what does that mean for each of us? Does anything or anyone matter?

Are you in a season of life where you are feeling so very alone with no known escape? You could be sharing days with hundreds of people but are devoid of a genuine heart connection with anyone or anything.

No one can deny that we live in a world of more uncertainty, turmoil, isolation, and hopelessness than ever before in history. The reality of our earthly existence is that things are a mess, so how can we really live? Why do we sometimes feel as if we are dying before we are dead?

Maybe you consider yourself greatly blessed; you have everything, yet something is still missing. The parties, sports, popularity, homes, cars, travel, friends, power, clothes, jewelry, fame, and lots of "stuff" are fun and nice, and certainly enhance our enjoyment of life, but it's not enough. You often wonder, *is that all there is?* Deep within our heart and soul we know there is something more.

The answer to all these is simple, yet profound: This life is *not* all there is!

All this world has to offer in material delight is not the substance of a purposeful, rewarding and genuinely fulfilling life. We may live in beautiful dwelling places or a shack, but where we live now is *not* our home. We are *not* home yet. If we consider home to be the location of all our stuff, no matter how much stuff we have, it will never be enough. Everyone agrees that home is where the heart is. Yet, home is not just the dwelling place of those with whom we share a heart connection on earth, but it also is *anywhere* we exist when Jesus is at home in our hearts.

God has set eternity in our hearts, therefore, what matters most in our temporary world is what matters most from an eternal perspective.

The world can try to satisfy that longing in your soul, but only Jesus can satisfy your soul. The material blessings in this world can be wonderful. God created this world for our delight and enjoyment, but if all we have is what this world offers, without the treasures of Heaven, then we only exist instead of genuinely live.

The richest and most famous man who ever lived was King Solomon. But everything in this world for him was still not enough. I can envision him as being much like the Mick Jagger of ancient days while wandering around in his magnificent golden castle singing:

"I can't get no satisfaction!" I think maybe Mick had gleaned inspiration from Solomon who wrote:

> *"Everything is meaningless," ...completely meaningless!" What do people get for all their hard work under the sun? Generations come and generations go, but the earth never changes. The sun rises and the sun sets, then hurries around to rise again. The wind blows south, and then turns north. Around and around it goes, blowing in circles. Rivers run into the sea, but the sea is never full. Then the water returns again to the rivers and flows out again to the sea. Everything is wearisome beyond description. No matter how much we see, we are never satisfied. No matter how much we hear, we are not content.*
> (Ecclesiastes 1:2-8, NLT)

Death is the ultimate destiny for ten out of ten people. It is a 100% probability, with the exception of those who will be taken without physical death at the Rapture. But we are not dead yet, so it may sound like an oxymoron to declare, "don't die before you're dead." However, if we are merely living for the pleasures of this world and/or not living as God created us to be, we can become as "walking dead people," joyless functioning humans with no real direction or purpose, and with a robotic attitude about all of life.

This book is to awaken your spirit to live with all your heart in being and becoming all God created you to be. It is not a study of all that happens when you die, or about prophecy concerning Jesus coming again, or about intricate details of Heaven. Also, it is not to expand upon the futility of the riches in this world.

I write about what happened before, during, and after I had died for more than 39 minutes. How it transformed my focus that no matter how old or young, rich or poor, in and through any and all situations, we can choose to live with a heart of joy and purpose. When God brought me back to life, it was not just to keep my physical heart beating, but to shock my spirit into realizing that life is truly worth living when we know, love, and serve the Lord. We are not to lose our passion to live, for God has destined us to fulfill His plan every day of our lives in mysterious ways that will bless us throughout eternity.

My testimony is to encourage you to know that you are not alone. We are assured of God's presence, power, and love to be and become all we were created for. As we put our trust in Him, nothing can be impossible to keep us fully alive, one day a time, until the day we close our eyes and open them in Heaven.

"Jesus looked at them and said, "With man this is impossible, but with God all things are possible." (Matthew 19:26, NIV)

This book is based on my testimony of the healing power of prayer in overcoming the impossibility of living after being physically dead. May my miracle inspire you to know that God, who began a good work in you, will be faithful to complete the beautiful and wonderful purpose of your life – and to do so with a heart of joy.

May my miracle inspire you also to embrace the eternal blessings of living with a heart of joy.

When facing impossibilities, I used to say that as long as there is life, there is hope. Now I can say with absolute certainty that even if there is not life, there is still hope.

A remarkable Bible teacher in the 1700's, George Whitefield, is best known for saying, *"…we are all immortal until our work on earth is done."*

My "Joy-Version" of his quote is, *"It ain't over until God sings it so!"*

"The Lord your God is with you, He is mighty to save you, He will rejoice over you with singing!" (Zephaniah 3:14-17)

God is not finished with you yet and He has given you a purpose that is so amazing, He composes a song over your life. The complications and challenges of daily responsibilities may often seem as troubling as a country music saga. However, now you only see in part of the song over you; one day you will fully know the beauty of the symphony of your life.

"In the same way, we can see and understand only a little about God now, as if we were peering at his reflection in a poor mirror; but someday we are going to see him in his completeness, face-to-face. Now all that I know is hazy and blurred, but then I will see everything clearly, just as clearly as God sees into my heart right now"
(I Corinthians 13:12).

Every ordinary day is created for the extraordinary when we trust in the Lord with all our hearts.

Your life matters, no matter who you are, no matter where you live, and no matter if you're living in abundance or lack.

Nothing in this world can compare to the blessings of God that are not of this world. That is why your life is not to be over until you hear the last concluding words of His melodious song for you in this temporary home. That is why you must discover what God created you for, and to do it for as long as you have life and breath on earth. What you do now will determine your eternal destiny.

You still have a lot of life to live before entering into the joy of the Lord, before the song of your life on earth is finished and the new song of eternal life has begun.

Your life may seem like an insignificant melody now, but one day you will know how God has worked all things together and He has created the most glorious masterpiece of musical joys through your choices in what is temporary, which assures you of eternal blessings more wondrous than you can imagine.

"And we know that God causes everything to work together for the good of those who love God and are called according to his purpose for them" (Romans 8:28).

The worst of life will become the best of life when you realize that your life matters to God. *"He has made everything beautiful in its time"* (Ecclesiastes 3:11, NIV). The beauty of life is best seen and experienced when living with a heart of joy, in realizing the Word of God is true for you!

Thank you for joining me in this journey of understanding the blessings of living with the joy of the Lord as your strength. I invite you to envision yourself walking with me while engaging in the events of my first 68 years of overwhelming challenges – including having died from a broken heart at age 66 and coming to life again more than 39 minutes later, returning to my mortal body and dwelling in the same fallen world, but with a renewed perspective to not die before I was dead (for good).

May God keep singing over your life until it is time for you to join the choirs of Heaven.

Life is short, don't die before you're dead!

Don't Die before You're Dead

"Teach us to number our days and recognize how few they are; help us to spend them as we should" (Psalm 90:11).

Dedicated to my daughter, Melody Joy, who saved my life through the power of the Holy Spirit; to my grandson, Carson, who watched me die and embraced the power of prayer to bring me back; to my grandson, Gavin, who prayed with unwavering faith in God's power and confidently declared God was not finished with me yet, I still had work to do; to my grandson, Theodore, whose life fills my heart with perpetual "Merry Heart Moments" that bring healing and a Heavenly perspective of life; and to all my dear family and others who faithfully petitioned the throne of Heaven for my recovery, knowing that with God ALL things are possible! And to joyful Dr. Brittany Owensby and other physicians and nurses in the ICU at Beaches Baptist Medical Center, Jacksonville Beach, FL, and Baptist Heart Health in Jacksonville, FL who did not give up on me.

CONTENTS

INTRODUCTION

I was DOA (dead on arrival) at a hospital for a documented 39 minutes! But I am not a "zombie," I am a living, breathing human.

I died in my daughter's car from sudden cardiac arrest, not just a mere heart attack, but an event called "the widow maker," because certain death always comes in only minutes. The arteries of my heart were 100% blocked.

My heart had stopped beating. My vital organs were starved of oxygen, and here's what that means:

After 1 minute of oxygen deprivation, brain cells begin to die, but survival is possible.

After 3 minutes, serious brain damage is likely.

After 10 minutes, many brain cells have died and the patient is unlikely to recover.

After 15 minutes, recovery is virtually impossible.

Yet nothing – absolutely nothing – is impossible with God!

Miraculously, my eternal soul returned to my mortal body, and I became alive again. Doctors refer to me as "a walking miracle," for there is no medical explanation for my recovery.

Only the power of healing and restoration, released through the petitions of countless prayer warriors, can explain the "how" of my miraculous recovery.

The reason I was alive again was that God was not finished with me yet.

"And I am sure that God who began the good work within you will keep right on helping you grow in his grace until his task within you is finally finished on that day when Jesus Christ returns" (Philippians 1:6).

This is my story. May it bless the story of your life!

"For I know the plans I have for you, says the Lord. They are plans for good and not for evil, to give you a future and a hope" (Jeremiah 29: 11).

Psalm 91

We live within the shadow of the Almighty, sheltered by the God who is above all gods.

This I declare, that he alone is my refuge, my place of safety; he is my God, and I am trusting him.

For he rescues you from every trap and protects you from the fatal plague. He will shield you with his wings! They will shelter you.

His faithful promises are your armor.

Now you don't need to be afraid of the dark anymore, nor fear the dangers of the day; nor dread the plagues of darkness, nor disasters in the morning.

Though a thousand fall at my side, though ten thousand are dying around me, the evil will not touch me.

I will see how the wicked are punished, but I will not share it.

For Jehovah is my refuge! I choose the God above all gods to shelter me. How then can evil overtake me or any plague come near?

For he orders his angels to protect you wherever you go.

They will steady you with their hands to keep you from stumbling against the rocks on the trail.

You can safely meet a lion or step on poisonous snakes, yes, even trample them beneath your feet!

For the Lord says, "Because he loves me, I will rescue him; I will make him great because he trusts in my name.

When he calls on me, I will answer; I will be with him in trouble and rescue him and honor him …I will satisfy him with a full life and give him my salvation."

Chapter 1

THE MORNING MY HEART

STOPPED BEATING

On the morning of April 23, 2022, it happened.

POUND...POUND…POUND…..

My daughter, Melody Joy, was initiating CPR by forcefully pounding on my chest with her right fist and continuing to drive with her left hand en route to Baptist Beaches Medical Center, Jacksonville Beach, Florida. With supernaturally charged intensity, she fearlessly attempted to restart my heart, crying out, "Jesus! Jesus! Jesus!" Melody was not screaming His name out of frustration or despair. She was crying out in passionate prayer to the great Physician, our Healer, our God, to deliver me from death.

In the seat behind me, my 7-year-old grandson, Carson, sat silently in shock and disbelief, having just witnessed me – his "G-Joy" – die. Yet he also folded his hands in prayer, realizing his "Aummy" (Aunt Mommy Melody Joy) was in a battle for my life.

This was a battle that must be won!

Just weeks before, I had been with Melody Joy when she purchased a new SUV. We joked about how the one she chose included a turbo charged engine. She normally preferred to drive slowly and cautiously, so we did not anticipate her ever activating the turbo boost of power to move swiftly through traffic. However, on that fateful morning, it was as if God had provided that very car for this "Jesus take the wheel" crisis.

Jesus, indeed, had to have taken the wheel, as it seems impossible that Melody could simultaneously drive, perform CPR, contact 911, call the hospital, and call her twin sister, Rachel, to pray with her. Together, my girls ignited a prayer chain that would ultimately reach countless prayer warriors throughout the world.

Melody had never been properly trained to do CPR, so she momentarily considered whether her efforts in the car were enough. Perhaps she should wait for an ambulance? Maybe she should pull me out of the car, lay me flat, and then push forcefully on my chest with both hands; everyone knows that's the proper way to perform CPR. Yet something in her heart told her to keep doing what she was doing, for I needed more than just CPR. In those critical moments, it was Melody's faith that supernaturally empowered her to not give up.

Melody had always been the first in our family to pray about everything – beginning when she could barely talk at 2 years of age and was asking God unceasingly to "heal Momma" after I'd had wisdom teeth removed. Melody was the first of my 3 children to pray for Jesus Christ to be her Lord and Savior when she was only 4 years old. Since then, she has witnessed the presence and power of God – through prayer – to overcome in countless hopeless and impossible situations. A lifetime of prayer had prepared her for such a time as this.

To witness someone faint and realize they may have died is so shocking that it often causes onlookers to momentarily freeze in fear and disbelief, but Melody did not hesitate for even a moment to immediately respond with prayer and action. Melody always tries to figure out a way when there seems to be no way. Doing nothing is never a consideration. She could not waste a precious second giving in to doubt or fear. She sensed prayers being answered as she felt the Holy Spirit guiding and strengthening her through every momentous decision.

"My mom died in my car… I'm almost to the hospital…. have someone there ready to help revive her!" Melody shouted to the one who'd answered the emergency phone at the hospital.

"You should stop and pull her out of the car to do CPR," was the eerily calm voice of the operator.

"I told you, we're almost there. Please have someone meet us!"

"Where are you exactly?"

Exasperated, Melody firmly responded, "On Penman, less than a mile away. Hurry!"

"Just stop where you are, we'll send an ambulance...."

"WHAT?"

Screeching to a halt at the hospital emergency entrance, she'd made it there so quickly, no one was yet outside.

She had to leave Carson alone in the hot car while running for help. Sweet 7-year-old Carson was briefly alone with the lifeless body of his G-Joy. Carson sat quietly in the hot car while feeling as if he were flying in outer space.

Melody burst through the doors and ran through the halls screaming for help.

Everything seemed to be moving in slow motion. Where was everyone? It seemed as if she was in the twilight zone. Mere moments seemed an infinity.

Two hospital workers responded to her frantic desperation.

"My mom has died," Melody shouted as she ran back to her car to continue CPR – with both hands – as the helpers followed behind with a wheelchair.

She again took charge with melodic and steady rhythms pushing on my chest and praying with every thrust.

"She needs a gurney!"

One hospital helper took over from Melody in administering CPR, while the other rushed away and momentarily returned with a gurney. The two who had responded to her pleas for help made a sincere, yet clumsy attempt to lift my limp body onto the gurney by grabbing only my arms and legs. Melody intervened by reaching under my torso with both her arms. With supernatural strength, she was able to lift me onto the gurney while the others ensured I was fastened securely upon it. All available doctors immediately responded to the "code blue" as my body had no breath, no heartbeat. I was rushed into the critical care unit.

Carson snuggled alongside Melody as they continued to pray together while following those who were rolling my lifeless body toward waiting doctors. They stood prayerfully outside the door while inside they implemented measures to stimulate my heart to beat again. Carson was amazingly calm and quiet during the frantic actions of everyone around him. He said he was not afraid but felt a little shaky. He had learned about the miraculous power of

God since he was a baby and now, at 7, he was in the midst of a crisis through which he would actually witness a genuine miracle.

Melody and I, and Carson's parents, Kevin and Rachel, have been dedicated to his spiritual growth from birth. Even before he was born, we prayed daily for him. For 7 years, we had been praying and reading the Bible with and for him, revealing to him and his brother Gavin how to know, love, and serve the Lord. Instead of church nurseries when they very young, they preferred to sit with us on the front rows of "big people" worship services. They sang the hymns with us and especially enjoyed finding Melody's place in the massive choir to sing along with her. During sermons they would color pictures of Bible stories. From their earliest memories, they have known through daily Biblical studies that our God is an awesome God who loves us, cares for us, is our best friend and is always with us!

Talking about God is a part of our daily conversations. We engage in prayer in and through all things. Prayer is not usually a "close-your-eyes-and-bow-your-head" activity for us; prayer is knowing we can talk to our Lord and Savior anytime, anywhere. Consequently, Gavin's and Carson's very young hearts were prepared to believe in the power of God that day to restore my damaged heart.

∞ ∞ ∞

All three of my grandsons have been the greatest joys of my life in my senior years. I have enjoyed countless adventures and opportunities to share life with them since they were born, and there was and is nothing in life I enjoy more. Since they were babies, my daily prayer for them is to be blessed mentally, physically, emotionally, vocationally and to be full of the joy of the Lord.

I've always called them "mighty warrior men of God" and encouraged them to embrace the promises of God's Word in all they do. It may seem strange to refer to a little boy as a "warrior" or "men of God," but I was making a prophetic proclamation as a foundation for their lives. My heart's desire has been/is always to help them be strong in the Lord and the power of His Might, to be boys who grow in wisdom, love, peace, goodness, patience, and kindness, to be and become all God created them to be as strong and wise leaders when they are men.

On April 23, 2022, Carson and Gavin were to discover that it wasn't just in Bible days that there were miracles. It wasn't just when Jesus was walking on the earth that He would heal people and even raise the dead. It wasn't just young Bible boys and men like David, Samuel, Daniel, and Joseph whose prayers God answered. For on *that* day, they would be a part of a miracle. All they had come to understand about being mighty warrior men of God, they were to fulfill in that moment.

They were used of God to help their G-Joy, (the name Gavin gave me when he was just 1 year old) through their faith and much prayer to not just be healed from a disease, but to overcome death.

As I think back upon the years before I was temporarily taken from their world, I assumed God would keep me alive until the Rapture with strength, joy, and sustained health long enough to actively be involved with my grandsons well into their adult years (if the Rapture were delayed). I could not even imagine the possibility I would not be alive in this world to witness them grow from boys loving Jesus into men of faith and favor with God and man.

Although I believe the Scriptures clearly reveal how those in Heaven can witness what happens on earth (i.e., Luke 15:7 and Hebrews 12:1), I did not want to watch their lives from the grandstands of Heaven; I wanted to be actively involved throughout all their lives on earth. As I prayed for God's will to be done for them on earth as it is in Heaven, it included me being on earth to experience it with them. Heaven is more wonderful than I can imagine, but I could not imagine going there until my work to fully and greatly bless Gavin, Carson, Theodore and any future grandchildren is complete. There was still much to do with and for my grandsons. So, Heaven could wait.

Also, our only opportunity to store up treasures in Heaven is through what we do on earth. Therefore, I did not want the time cut short to do so, not just for me, but also to help demonstrate and share with my grandsons how we are to live on earth for what matters most in Heaven.

"Don't store up treasures here on earth where they can erode away or may be stolen. Store them in heaven where they will never lose their value and are safe from thieves. If your profits are in heaven, your heart will be there too" (Matthew 6:19-21).

My heart's desire was to share with my grandsons their joys and tears, hopes and dreams, successes and failures, just as I have with my adult children. While growing older can often put limitations on our physical bodies, there are no limits on how we can bless our grandchildren through our God-ordained heart connection.

So, for God to bring me back to a full life on earth, He has done for me what he promised in Psalm 37:4: *"Be delighted with the Lord. Then he will give you all your heart's desires."*

My heart's desires are to share many more inspirational conversations with Gavin and to watch him discover what he loves to do and become the best at it. I want to laugh and play challenging games with him, to witness his excellence at tennis competitions and all he pursues, to watch him one day becoming a builder, business owner, husband, dad and maybe even governor of Florida – whatever is the fulfillment of his heart's desires.

My heart desires to hear more of Carson's jokes and have fun with him, and to watch him be and become the best God created him to be. I want to delight over his funny and amazing talents in tennis competitions, to witness his engaging "warrior" spirit in all of life. Since he was very little, he has loved wearing "warrior" costumes and "fighting the bad guys" with his "sword of the Spirit." I want to witness his warrior spirit destroying attacks of the enemy as he matures, and watch him maybe be a doctor one day. Most definitely, I want to see him fulfill what he's told us is the desire of his heart: "to grow up and get married so he can protect his family."

I want to laugh and play much more with Theo (whom I also call "Theodorable"). My heart longs to experience more of his dancing, singing, entertaining talents and joyful delight in everything. I want to watch him learn to read, grow in knowledge and wisdom, and be and become all God created him to be, discovering what he loves to do and becoming the best at it. I want to love and care for and teach the love of Jesus to all my future grandchildren.

My heart's desire is to help guide my grandsons to know that God will bless them with their hearts' desires, when they put their trust in Him and obey His Word, including the following in Proverbs:

"When a man is trying to please God, God makes even his worst enemies to be at peace with him. ......We should make plans—counting on God to direct us" (Proverbs 16:7-9).

"How much better is wisdom than gold, and understanding than silver!

The path of the godly leads away from evil; he who follows that path is safe.

Pride goes before destruction and haughtiness before a fall.

Better poor and humble than proud and rich.

God blesses those who obey him; happy the man who puts his trust in the Lord.

The wise man is known by his common sense, and a pleasant teacher is the best.

Wisdom is a fountain of life to those possessing it, but a fool's burden is his folly.

From a wise mind comes careful and persuasive speech.

Kind words are like honey—enjoyable and healthful.

Before every man there lies a wide and pleasant road he thinks is right, but it ends in death" (Proverbs 16:16-25).

To fully understand my heart miracle is to recognize the "grandson factor" that I am convinced was most significant to bring me back to life.

Somewhere in my consciousness, when my spirit and soul were absent from my body, I believed that the heart connection I had with my grandsons would help my heart start beating again.

My grandsons were a vital part of a miracle that not only changed my life, but also would change the rest of their lives.

Grandparents are ordained to help teach our grandchildren of the greatness and power of God. Parents set the foundation for children to learn of salvation through Jesus Christ and grandparents provide encouragement and prayer support to ensure children realize all that God desires for their lives.

I rejoiced with Rachel and Kevin when Carson and Gavin were born, but even more so when they were each born again when they were 4 years old, the same age I was when I trusted in Jesus as my Lord and Savior, and the same age as their momma and aummy when they were saved. When Gavin was 5 years old, he asked me to baptize him in the kiddie pool at their club by the Atlantic Ocean on a most glorious day. Carson also asked me to baptize him in that same kiddie pool. I joyfully and tearfully baptized my grandsons who, years later, would pray for my life to be restored because they knew it was not my time to die. I enthusiastically anticipate the day when Theodore also is born again – and already rejoice in how he says he "loves Jesus," and prays to "keep mean kids away on the playground," and how he delights in learning Bible verses and singing Bible songs. Any time we're together, I make time to help him grow in wisdom and knowledge of the Lord.

Teaching Gavin, Carson and Theodore about how much God loves them, God likes them, and has a wonderful plan for their lives has not only included regularly reading the Bible with and to them, but also through their gleaning spiritual wisdom and understanding from reading Bible-infused books, watching inspirational videos and programs together, such as *Bibleman©*, *Owlegories©*, *Superbook©*, *Kids Sing Praise©*, *McGee and Me©*, *Davey and Goliath©*, *Seakids©*, and movies about real life families who trusted in God through overwhelming challenges, such as Dolly Parton's family portrayed in her movie, *Coat of Many Colors©*, and the Von Trapp family in *The Sound of Music©*.

On that fateful Spring morning in April 2022, Carson and Gavin were living through what seemed to be surreal moments of their own family's real life movie.

My grandsons were connected to my heart before it stopped beating. They were still connected after my heart stopped beating. God was preparing me in the most profound way to be an even greater blessing to my grandchildren than I ever could have been before.

∞ ∞ ∞

"CODE BLUE"

Standing outside the door of the critical care unit at the Baptist Beaches hospital, Melody heard confirmation that I was officially DEAD. My soul was on the edge of eternity.

Chapter 2

FULLY ALIVE THEN SUDDENLY DEAD

O ften, people ask if I'd had any symptoms or felt bad any time before cardiac failure, but the day before I died, I was fully alive. In fact, I was fully alive and enjoying a most wonderful day with Carson after auditioning for a commercial job. I cheered him on during his tennis competition from the afternoon until early evening. After tennis, it had become chilly and windy, but he was not bothered by the cold winds and asked to have dinner at an outdoor restaurant by the beach across from the tennis courts.

It was extra delightful to be with Carson that evening as he shared lots of new jokes, amusing stories, and mischievous adventures. I remember one funny story Carson told me about catching lizards and giving them names. We kept warm covering up with beach towels while eating mac-n-cheese and pizza. We also enjoyed looking for dolphins and sharks that might be frolicking in the ocean waves. My time with Carson the night before I died had been energizing and extra special.

I don't often get to enjoy time alone with each of my three grandsons anymore, but when I do, it's the best time of my life. Their love of life, their desire to know about God and Jesus, the Holy Spirit and the Bible, coupled with their inquisitive natures and views of the world from such pure and innocent perspectives are all wellsprings of blessing and joy to my heart. They are not only fun, funny and interesting to be around, but also they are a perpetual reminder of what is most important in life, and what is not. All three of my grandsons are as Heaven on earth to me. Through them, I see and experience love as God created love to be.

After dinner, I took Carson to Melody's home where he was spending the night. Through the years we'd prepare for bed by first having a little dance party to such songs as *Choose Joy*© by King and Country, or *Prayer Anthem*© by Carman. Dancing to those vigorous and dynamic inspirational songs not only helped Carson and Gavin expend any extra energy and more quickly fall asleep, but also put good thoughts into their minds for happy dreams. That particular night, however, Carson was already very tired after a long and busy day and he didn't need a dance party to be ready to go to sleep. In lieu of dancing, we read one of our favorite Bible passages, Psalm 91, which I have encouraged Gavin and Carson commit to memory. Carson's favorite verses :

"For Jehovah is my refuge! I choose the God above all gods to shelter me. How then can evil overtake me or any plague come near? For he orders his angels to protect you wherever you go. They will steady you with their hands to keep you from stumbling against the rocks on the trail. You can safely meet a lion or step on poisonous snakes, yes, even trample them beneath your feet! (Psalm 91:9-13).

We then prayed for all our family, for friends, for our dogs, and for happy dreams. We gave thanks for the good things of the day we'd shared together, and we asked for God to bless the next day.

Carson asked me to tell him a "Charlie" story until he went to sleep. Since he and Gavin were toddlers, they have always enjoyed these stories that I made up about the adventures of a boy named Charlie who loved Jesus. My stories include how God helped Charlie through encounters with danger, confrontations with mean kids, involvement in sports, school, travel, meeting people from distant lands, and adventures in his ordinary life with family and friends. My "Charlie" stories are ever changing to relate to whatever Gavin and Carson are interested in. So, that night I told an original story about Charlie and baseball since Melody and I were to be taking Carson to his baseball game in the morning.

I consider bedtime stories one of the most important and fun duties of a grandma. Often, the content of bedtime stories remains in their thoughts throughout the night. My stories are to encourage my grandsons to know, without a doubt, that God loves them, God likes them, and has a wonderful plan for each of their lives. They've asked me for years to write these stories in a series of books so they can read them when I'm not with them, and so they can read them to their children one day. I had always assumed I had lots of years left to put the adventures of Charlie in writing. "Someday," was always my answer.

Since Carson had yet to drift off to sleep after the Charlie story, he asked me to sing a few songs.

Gavin and Carson have told me that my singing and/or playing inspirational songs and hymns on a CD or radio as they were falling asleep kept them from having nightmares. I'd written melodies to many scripture songs while singing to my children when they were growing up and continued this joyous tradition since the moment I first held Gavin, Carson and Theodore and gazed into their "heavenly eyes."

During their early years, Gavin and Carson always wanted me to sing them to sleep, but now that they are both "big boys," they have become too old to ask me to do so. Most often they ask Alexa to play K-LOVE™ instead. So, for Carson to ask me to sing to him that night and include *Awesome God*©, one of his favorite songs since he was about 2, was an especially cherished blessing. Teaching children to know, love, and serve the Lord has been a lifetime calling, and now, during my "senior years," there truly is nothing I enjoy more. Nor are there any things I consider more important for me to engage in than working alongside my adult children to help my grandchildren be and become all God created them to be. But I most certainly could never have imagined what would transpire after that night of singing and telling stories. In just hours, Carson would realize, more than ever, just how much our God IS an awesome God!

It was about 9PM when I left Melody's house. She was planning to pick me up about 8AM the next morning to go "treasure hunting" at community garage sales in my neighborhood before watching Carson's baseball game. That night, my sweet doggy daughter, Karly, was anxiously awaiting our nightly walk that was much later than usual. Just as any times shared with my grandsons were always the most joyful and blessed moments of any day, so was any precious moment with Karly. At 12, Karly was considered an old dog, but she acted like a puppy. Since she seemed to me to be so vibrantly alive I was in perpetual denial that Karly could ever possibly be old enough to cross the "rainbow bridge."

It was just me and Karly living together, since my other dear doggy children: Happy (who was my best friend for 17 years), and Kiwi (Melody's dog who had lived with me) had both crossed that bridge in recent years. Only dog lovers can understand that we never quite recover from the loss of our beloved pets. However, I have some consolation in personally believing we'll see our pets again in Heaven. It just seems logical that since they were as "Heaven on earth" to us, they also will end up in Heaven with us one day.

Billy Graham said: "*Heaven will be a place of perfect happiness for us—and if we need animals around us to make our happiness complete, then you can be sure God will have them there.*" (https://billygraham.org/answer/i-suppose-youve-been-asked-this-before-but-will-there-be-)

Just two years before, in 2020, only three months after losing Kiwi, and one year after Happy was gone, Karly became paralyzed. She could not move nor even bark. God knew that my heart could not stand losing her. He made a way where there seemed to be no way for her to receive lifesaving spinal fusion surgery. I'd been referring to her ever since as "Miracle Karly," for she not only survived the microscopic surgery, but thrived. Within a week after having been paralyzed, she was playing and running as if nothing had ever happened. Miracle Karly's companionship and love during the challenging months of the Covid-related lockdowns and other major concerns were essential for my own emotional health and healing. Dog lovers can fully understand the mystery of this canine therapeutic power.

Walking with Karly that night before I died was extra peaceful and joyous. The stars were shining with magnified brilliance. As we walked alongside it, the reflection of the moon was "painting" the waves of a nearby pond, resembling twinkling diamonds. Just as in Heaven there is "perfect" love, the love of a dog can seem like a reflection of Heavenly love. Perhaps Adam gave the name "dog" for our canine companions because to read it backwards, it spells "God." I say this of course in jest, but Karly in my life was a constant reminder of God's faithful and enduring love, and I cherished every moment with her in my life.

Just as God is closest to us when we are in most need of comfort, so Karly had been for me, consoling me through sorrow, playing with me when I was happy, cuddling on my lap when I was glad or sad. Karly was my faithful friend; walking with her was always one of the simple pleasures of life that gave me the greatest joys.

"I sure do love you, Karly. Please don't ever die," I said to her after she'd jumped on my lap to rest a bit on a park bench and gaze at the stars. She wagged her tail, looking at me with a smile and twinkles in her eyes that always pierced my heart with such joy. I could never have imagined the walk with Karly the night before I died would be our last walk together in this world. It never crossed my mind that any walk would be our last.

It's rather interesting that just weeks before that final walk with Karly, Carson had asked me who would take care of Karly if I died. My response was a hopeful declaration that neither of us was going to die. Since Happy and Kiwi were no longer with me, surely God would allow Karly to stay until the Rapture. And I sure wasn't anticipating dying anytime soon. Carson had never asked such a deeply concerning question about Karly or inquired regarding my death before. Why had he done so then? It's almost as if he'd had a premonition of something about to happen.

The last time I'd been together with Carson, Gavin, Melody, Rachel and Kevin was six days before I died, on Easter, Resurrection Sunday. Just six days after celebrating the resurrection of Jesus, I was myself to experience a personal "resurrection." During that family gathering, Carson had entertained all of us through his enthusiasm to capture eggs at the annual Easter egg hunt on the beach. After he failed to find the "golden" egg, we stayed at the beach a while, sharing some golden moments, enthralled by fascinating cloud formations indicating a rather ominous storm approaching. Since it was speedily moving in our direction, we walked to a restaurant to take photos under a safe covering from rain. Gavin and Carson were wearing their peach-colored Easter suits, so we were enthusiastically taking as many photos of them as they would allow.

At the moment Rachel snapped a shot of me with my gorgeous grandsons, lighting struck dangerously close. The exploding and deafening sound, coupled with the alarming sight of electrical power piercing the ground within just a few hundred feet, caused the boys to scream and my heart to beat extra hard and fast. Rachel's picture captured the shocked expressions on Gavin's and Carson's faces at the exact moment of the strike. None of us had ever been in such close proximity to an explosive lightning strike.

Could that shocking moment have been a harbinger of another never before experienced event that was to occur just days later? It sure seemed as if something changed in the way I felt in my heart on Resurrection Sunday. The electrically charged atmosphere caused my heart to flutter a little longer than I would have expected. Just six days later, a uniquely powerful bolt of electricity was to pierce my flesh with the shock of my life!

That Friday night, about 11PM, April 22, 2022, I closed my eyes after Karly jumped up on the bed and rested her white, fluffy head on my left foot. My eyes did not open again with conscious awareness until the following

Wednesday morning, April 27th. Everything I've written that happened during those five days is from the accounts told me by Melody Joy, my family, doctors, and others who were with me as I left this world of the living …died... and came back to life on earth.

I do not remember waking up on Saturday morning, April 23, 2022. I do not remember getting dressed. I do not remember sending a group text to all my children. I do not remember calling Melody Joy and telling her to come right away because I didn't feel well and needed to go to the hospital. I do not remember taking care of Karly in the morning, going downstairs and sitting on the curb waiting for Melody and Carson. I do not remember putting on my seat belt. I do not remember Melody calling 911. I do not remember Melody calling on others to pray. I do not recall chest pain. I do not remember vomiting. I do not remember any of those crucial hours or minutes preceding my death.

Melody told me that just as she and Carson were about to leave her home, I had sent a group text to her, Rachel, my son Daniel and his wife Gabi, with pictures of two bottles of herbal supplements. I'd consumed a dosage of each the night before and in the morning. The instructions on the bottles were to take a few drops under the tongue of Vitamins K and D3 and MCT oil. I don't remember why I had these herbs. It's almost as if subconsciously I was aware "something" was wrong because these were all vitamins and herbs known to be beneficial for the heart and circulatory system. I don't remember why I'd even thought to purchase these heart supplements before that day. I also sent a picture of the insert in the box of the herbs that stated: "Get ready to feel the best you've ever felt." We can't help but laugh now about that claim.

There is no way of knowing if the herbal drops I'd taken before I died were in any way responsible for my sudden cardiac arrest and death. It could have just been a coincidence. I just know that I took them only hours before I died and felt it important enough to send pictures to my children.

Carson snuggled closely against Melody as they stood just outside the door of the critical care unit when Melody called his dad, Kevin. He was already en route to the hospital to begin his rounds as a physician there. Initially, his heart skipped a beat when hearing Carson was at the hospital with her. Relieved to learn of Carson's well-being, he naturally was concerned about me. Kevin didn't normally work on Saturdays. For him to be working there on that particular Saturday was a Divine appointment. His presence within minutes of Melody's call was needed to care for Carson and consult with medical staff....and for expanding the domain of prayer support.

He had only been with Melody and Carson momentarily when a physician on duty offered condolences to Kevin because I had died. Kevin called Rachel to tell her that her mom was dead.

Melody would not leave her position of prayer outside my room where life had yet to return to my body. She could hear the conversations… the "code blue." She could hear ten times, "clear," "clear," clear", "clear" as the staff used a single pair of defibrillators attempting to ignite a charge in my withered heart.

Normal procedure to resuscitate someone from unconsciousness or "coded" is no more than three or four times, but my doctors were not normal; they were being supernaturally inspired to not give up. Passionate and fervent prayers were bombarding the throne of Heaven.

Help was on the way!

Chapter 3

ALIVE AGAIN?

"We are immortal until our work on earth is done."
George Whitfield

"Is she really gone?" That was the lingering question during those more than 39 minutes in the twilight zone with my wandering soul suspended in some unknown dimension between time and space.

As doctors passionately fought to ignite a breath into my lifeless body, Melody called her twin sister, Rachel, who was five hours away in South Florida where Gavin was competing in a tennis tournament. Before Kevin had informed Rachel that I was *"already gone,"* she and Gavin continued praying on their knees, weeping and passionately pleading with God to save my life. They prayed because they knew in their hearts that it's not over until God says it's over. For those praying for me, death was not an option. Life was infused in their prayers.

When confronted with fearful situations throughout my life, I have declared, "As long as there's life, there's hope," but now I can honestly and confidently shout that even when there is no life, there is still hope. Something happens when prayers bombard the throne of God, something that unleashes power beyond what our finite minds can comprehend, or mere science can explain.

"...pray for each other so that you may be healed. The earnest prayer of a righteous man has great power and wonderful results" (James 5:16).

In my "Joy Version," this Bible verse means the following: "Pray passionately. Pray with all your heart, soul, body and mind! If Jesus is your Lord and Savior, then you have access to the greatest power in all the universe – the King of Kings, Lord of Lords and the Master of the Universe who created humans to pray."

Through our mortal prayers, God has chosen to fulfill His Will on earth. I still don't completely understand why and how God has chosen mere mortals to fulfill His Divine purposes. I just know that He DOES! Perpetually praying is to know perpetual power.

"Always be joyful. Never stop praying. Be thankful in all circumstances, for this is God's will for you who belong to Christ Jesus" (I Thessalonians 5:16-18).

The prayers were not to stop. As long as there was prayer, there was hope even in death.

∞ ∞ ∞

Melody, Rachel, Gavin, Carson, Daniel, Kevin, Gabi, Theo, my best friend Claire, and countless other righteous people prayed for me. Some I knew and loved, others I just barely knew, and most I did not know at all. The power of saints united in prayer touched the throne of God and dispatched a mighty force in the unseen world to ignite a miracle that resulted in something unimaginably wonderful.

Rachel and Gavin were weeping and praying together on their knees upon hearing that "something bad" had happened, when Gavin stood up with confidence and unwavering strength and faith and declared, "I'm not crying anymore. G-Joy is not going to die. God is not finished with her yet. She still has things to do. It is not her time to die. She's gonna be alright."

And then something happened in the critical care unit of Baptist Beaches Medical Center. This "something" was a force not visible through human eyes. A Heaven-sent response to prayer fell upon the determined doctors who refused to give up on the fight to save my life. A rush of an electrifying explosion of insight and purpose surged through those medical warriors, inspiring a determination to utilize all available ordinary physical resources in a most extraordinary, supernatural way.

Melody overheard someone with me in the critical emergency care room say, "Let's double it."

This confident command was from a young woman I will refer to as "Dr. Find-A-Way," for she was used of God to find a way when there seemed to be no way. She instructed the medical team to use double defibrillators at once. Two defibrillators, four electrical shock paddles, were quickly and strategically positioned on my battered torso. This procedure is so rare that no known person in that hospital had ever witnessed it; most did not even realize it to be a possibility.

The command was given: "CLEAR!"

And then …and then …a faint heartbeat …a breath …another breath …

God infused resurrection power into my heart to beat again. My eternal soul returned to my mortal flesh. I was alive again on Earth. It was 9:02AM. The records indicate my lifeless body had officially been admitted DOA to the hospital at 8:23AM. For at least 39 minutes, I had no breath, no heartbeat. For 39 minutes no oxygen had ignited life into any cell of my body.

I was *DEAD*....but now *ALIVE!*

It was a miracle!

The petitions spoken by mere mortals to Jehovah Rapha, and the healing power of the Blood of Jesus, had given me new life! I was kept from the grave! Through these prayers, the power of God from Heaven was unleashed upon men and machines on earth to restore life, igniting inspiration to do what *none* there had done before.

Nearly everyone is familiar with the use of defibrillators. They have been installed for easy access in almost all places where there are large gatherings, including sports arenas, malls, airports, schools, etc.

I learned how to use one myself when training to be a flight attendant. But in my training, there was never mention of a situation warranting the use of double defibrillators. In fact, it was taught that the shock of one defibrillator is so powerful that bystanders are to stand clear of heart attack victim. It was unimaginable to me to think that two used simultaneously would ever be a consideration.

But I had been dead far too long. They had exhausted the maximum use for trying to use one defibrillator. Obviously, one had not been enough. Therefore, there was nothing to lose and everything possibly to gain when responding to the Holy Spirit's inspiration to realize new meaning to a Bible verse that I often quote at weddings:

> *"...two are better than one..."* (Ecclesiastes 4:9 KJV).

During the weeks following that fateful event, I learned that the doctors who would not give up fighting to save my physical life also had been engaged in fighting a spiritual battle when silently praying for me and for each other. The team of medical warriors had been orchestrated by the Holy Spirit to be at that emergency room at that very time.

A most notable proof of this is when learning Dr Find-A-Way had just begun her career as a physician and was not supposed to be there that day. She had been assigned to Baptist South hospital and was on her way there when called to go to Baptist Beaches instead. She reported for duty in the ER just before Melody came to a stop outside. Days after I became conscious, she visited me at Baptist Heart Hospital and told me how she was a believer in Jesus Christ and had grown up attending First Baptist Church of Jacksonville, which I had also attended when I moved to Florida, and with Gavin and Carson in their younger years. She confirmed how the miracle was life changing for her, as it was for everyone there that day. She knew that God had blessed me with a miracle.

God calls His children into ministry in every profession. I'm eternally grateful that those with me that day had responded to God's call to work in the medical ministry. No doubt, they were doing what God created them for. They were truly Heaven-sent physicians and nurses. He brought that team together through the unseen power of fervent warrior prayer which transformed them into what I consider to be "Miracle Medical Warriors." They excelled at using their talents and skills to the best of their abilities. Indeed, their lives and mine would never be the same. When we all get to Heaven, I'm going to invite them to my mansion for a celebration party as Jesus reveals to all of us just how it happened!

I don't know if everyone in that critical care room shared the faith of my heart. I am certain and deeply grateful that God had prepared the hearts of those who were there to be united in their determination to restore my heart.

As I ponder this medical miracle story with the use of double defibrillators, I am reminded how on every jet plane I worked on as a flight attendant, I prayed that no one would ever need me to use a defibrillator. But, if it were to be necessary, I prayed for strength and wisdom to not hesitate in utilizing it correctly and effectively. If by using just one, I'd been able to bring someone back to life, I would have considered it a miracle. To use two was absolutely unbelievable!

And it was not just the double defibrillators, doctors, nurses, and machines that were to be miraculously utilized that day. It began with the awe-inspiring response of my daughter in reaction to the death of her mom. It especially was the way she was empowered to drive her car and calmly, yet with supernatural strength, she also was able to use just one fist to initiate CPR in a perfectly amazing way that sustained enough blood flow to my heart to give hope to doctors that there could be hope for me. What a wonderful Miracle Day!

∞ ∞ ∞

I still remember the verses I had memorized as a child about praying for the sick, and always believed God could heal anyone. On Wednesday nights every week when I was growing up in Ohio, our family would go to prayer meetings at church and nearly all requests were for someone to be healed. But I never recall a church service when anyone who was sick and being prayed for was healed. Yet the Bible is clear that faith and prayer will heal.

"And the prayer offered in faith will make the sick person well; the Lord will raise them up.... pray for each other so that you may be healed. The prayer of a righteous person is powerful and effective" (James 5:15-16).

Even though I never witnessed a healing in a church service, several times when I was in the hospital praying for my mom and my husband in hopeless situations, they *were* healed from specific concerns. This happened when there were "two or more in agreement" and when "laying hands on them," for that is what we're told to do in God's Word.

"I also tell you this—if two of you agree down here on earth concerning anything you ask for, my Father in heaven will do it for you. For where two or three gather together because they are mine, I will be right there among them" (Matthew 18:19-20).

Jesus promised his disciples that because He rose from the grave we have access to His power when we pray in His Name, including healing:

"...they will be able to place their hands on the sick and heal them" (Mark 16:18).

There are many passages in Scripture that instruct us to lay hands on the sick. There are also instructions to anoint them with oil when praying for their healing:

"Are any of you sick? You should call for the elders of the church to come and pray over you, anointing you with oil in the name of the Lord" (James 5:14 NLT).

The Bible refers to believers as "royal priesthood," so "elders" of a specific church are not the only ones who are ordained to place hands on the sick and pray for them. Anyone in whom the Holy Spirit dwells, who prays with faith in the name of Jesus our Healer, is qualified to do so. So, when praying for my mom, my husband and I laid hands on her; when praying for my husband, my daughters and I anointed him with oil and prayed for him. We merely did what God says to do. And each time, my mom and husband got better in ways the doctor's said they would not.

When I first became a chaplain, I was called to visit a little girl in the hospital who was in a coma. It was a daunting task. I knew to pray for healing. However, my Baptist background sometimes conflicted with what I believed the Bible teaches about healing, such as "laying hands on the sick and anointing them with oil." Since I had even been a student at a Baptist Seminary after graduating from a state university, I had been exposed to a lot of Baptist theology that naturally affected my perspective of the supernatural. But when I visited that precious little girl, I didn't draw from just what is considered mere traditional Baptist teachings, but from the foundation of all evangelical church theology that confirms that *all* the Bible is the Word of God, which I believe with all my heart. So, I knew that if God says to lay hands on someone sick, then I was to do it. However, when preparing to pray for the little girl, it would be my first time considering laying hands in prayer upon someone I did not personally know. It did not matter; I immediately dismissed thoughts I know were from the enemy that to do so would not be "proper." As I laid my hand on her shoulder, I felt empowered to pray for her to be healed and live a rich and full life.

Sometimes when we pray, our faith is not as strong as we feel it needs to be, especially when someone is very sick. However, it is not our faith that heals, for just a seemingly inadequate faith in Jesus to heal is more than enough. Even when we have the utmost faith, it is still only Jesus who saves, heals and delivers. And even though we don't always realize the outcome of our healing prayers as we think should happen, and truly believe the sick will be healed, we are only called to pray and trust and have faith in God's perfect will to be fulfilled. We must believe more like the simply profound faith of a child with the attitude: *of course God can.* And we must pray with the assurance that God will work any outcome for good for those who love Him and are called according to His purposes (Romans 8:28). I am absolutely certain that if we do not pray, then we can be assured things will not be the best.

When I was a chaplain and was called to pray for that little girl who was thought to be incurable, nothing seemed to have changed. I prayed for and encouraged her parents while continuing to pray for her after I left. Yet, I was discouraged and wept for I did not understand why God would not heal her. God gave me peace that there will always be things we don't understand in this world, but that does not mean He is not working through our prayers. One day, we will understand; sometimes we will know why things happen as they do in this world, but sometimes we will not know until we see Jesus.

Just after arriving home, I got a call, "She's awake, she's gonna be alright!" It was from this precious little girl's mom.

∞ ∞ ∞

The use of double defibrillators reminds me of the dual powers revealed on that miracle morning when the power of man and medicine merged with the power of faith and prayer. It was faith and prayer that empowered Melody to generate sufficient thrusts to my chest cavity to stimulate enough flow of blood to sustain me until I was under the care of a medical team. Faith and prayer empowered men and machines to do what could not be realized if the two powers were not interconnected. Although, God could have revived me from the dead without men or machines, God chooses to bestow great blessings upon those who are a great blessing. We are blessed to do the work of God on earth, and when we allow God to use us to bless others, we are the most blessed. Understanding years ago that we cannot always choose to be blessed, but we can always choose to be a blessing, motivated me to live by what I refer to as "joyisms." To me, this is defined as anything that encourages us to have a joyful heart. One of my first "joyisms" was "To be blessed, be a blessing"—TBBBAB.

Throughout my heart miracle, countless others would be greatly blessed as they greatly blessed me. The blessings were both spiritual and physical. This is what it means to have a blessed life.

Some people can seem to be too scientifically minded to consider the spiritual factor, while others can be too spiritually minded to consider the scientific factor.

We acknowledge that God created every substance in the world through which all things are molded into useful purposes. So, just as He inspired the invention of amazing medical devices, He certainly inspires how to use them most effectively. Therefore, it's only natural for medicine and machines to be most effective in health care and healing when there is also the powerful presence of faith and prayers.

Each of us has the option of choosing medicine with or without prayer and faith. I am thankful for those with me during a seemingly impossible crisis to have chosen what I know is best: prayer and faith-infused medicine.

∞ ∞ ∞

During the year it has taken me to write this book, and think deeply about all that happened, I am constantly seeking for a deeper understanding of the "why" and "what for" of it all.

I'll never fully understand it all until I get to talk to Jesus one day in my Heavenly home. I have considered that perhaps the shock of my miracle was to awaken a better understanding that since we live in the midst of increasingly shocking events in this world, we need not fear, for God is with us and for us. Our first response to a crisis is to try to figure it out on our own, but we must take to heart that, "God's got this."

There is no other way to explain what happened on that morning of April 23, 2022 – except with two words – **Only God**!

Only God can give us hope in the midst of hopelessness.

> *"Let him have all your worries and cares, for he is always thinking about you and watching everything that concerns you"* (I Peter 5:7).

I remember in the early 1970s as a teenager, first hearing Bill and Gloria Gaither's song, *Because He Lives*©, and knowing in my heart that this prevailing Biblical theme so beautifully put to music would be the focus of my life for decades before my heart miracle.

> Because He lives, I can face tomorrow, because He lives all fear is gone, because I know, I know He holds the future, life is worth the living just because He lives.

And so, too, the old hymn *He Lives*© has new meaning for the rest of my life after my miracle:

> I serve a risen Savior, He's in the world today;
> I know that he is living, whatever men may say.

I see His Hand of mercy, I hear His voice of cheer; and just the time I need Him, He's always near.

He Lives, He Lives, Christ Jesus Lives today.

He walks with me and talks with me, along life's narrow way.

He Lives, He Lives, Salvation to impart.

You ask me how I know He Lives?

He lives within my heart. (Alfred H Ackley, 1887-1960)

Chapter 4

SOUL AND BODY REUNITED, AND IT'S FEELING GOOD!

I know the LORD is always with me....
I will not be shaken, for He is right beside me
No wonder **MY HEART IS GLAD**-*and I rejoice!*
My body rests in safety.
For **YOU WILL NOT LEAVE MY SOUL AMONGST THE DEAD**
...or allow faithful one to rot in the grave.
YOU WILL SHOW ME THE WAY OF LIFE,
granting me the **JOY OF YOUR PRESENCE**
...and the pleasures of living with **YOU FOREVER** (Psalm 16:8-11, emphasis added).

When my eternal soul returned to my mortal body, I was intubated and connected to other life support mechanisms to prepare my transport from Baptist Beaches to Baptist Heart Hospital in downtown Jacksonville, Florida. My caregivers determined that a helicopter was the best option to expedite the transfer to heart specialists and surgeons, but time was of the essence to ensure my heart would keep beating. Just to know my heart had been reignited with steady beats was the first part of my miracle, but in the days ahead, this miraculous impact would be magnified.

Just as God sent exceptional doctors to be a part of the "Beaches Miracle," so I also believe He sent an ambulance to be immediately available to transfer me. One from another county had "coincidentally" showed up to the Beaches Hospital just after I'd come back to life. The ambulance would expedite my transport to the critical care heart specialists much faster than waiting for a helicopter.

41

Melody watched as I was transferred into the ambulance. It was then that the reality of all that had happened became vividly clear to her. She could no longer hold back the tears. Weeping and emotionally exhausted, she was in awe and wonder at what God had done.

I have often referred to Melody as my "golden girl" since she has come through countless "fires of life" as a shining testimony of God's power and faithfulness. Her golden faith had strengthened her to be ready for all that happened on that miracle day. She's still my golden girl, but I also now refer to her as "Miracle Melody." Miracles and angels were to surround me in abundance during my resurrection journey.

Miracle Melody was unable to accompany me in the ambulance. Kevin returned to his duties at the hospital, so she took Carson to his baseball game. Melody and Carson needed some normal moments to begin recovering from the trauma. Melody also found good friends to take care of my precious Karly.

Upon arrival at the Baptist Heart Hospital, doctors discovered that my main coronary artery was 100% blocked. They performed a balloon angioplasty and implanted a stent. That means they threaded a catheter with a balloon on the end into the blocked artery and inflated the balloon to enlarge the blocked area; the stent, a small tube, was implanted to ensure the restored blood flow continued. I had developed pneumonia in both lungs and was administered powerful drugs to sustain my life and control pain. My left arm was swollen twice it's normal size because of massive blood clots. IV's were in my neck, ankles and arms. I was alive, but it was uncertain whether I would ever again be truly living. My identification bracelet was on my ankle. Isn't that where they put it on a corpse? But I was no longer dead.

The cause of my death from a heart condition is nearly as much a mystery as it is to try to logically explain my resurrection. I never had high blood pressure, never smoked, never used illegal drugs, rarely had alcohol, and never had diabetes. I ate healthy most of the time (except for occasional treat of sweets, especially Haagen-Dazs® vanilla ice cream), I was physically active and in exceptionally good health, especially for my age. I did not have any known inherited tendencies for heart problems from my parents or grandparents, however, my two older sisters had heart attacks. Thankfully, one survived, but sadly, one did not. Sister Susan's cardiac event was especially significant for it happened when she was alone and could not reach a phone for emergency services. God's hand was on her life to sustain her as she lay bloody on the floor for six hours until her daughter, Pam, discovered her. Even though my sisters had heart issues, I had never seriously considered that I could be at risk.

As I reflect upon all that was to transpire, I have considered that perhaps God had prepared my physical heart to possess the strength and composition to be revived because of my lifetime of spiritually trusting in the Lord with all of my heart. Since the spirit and body are interconnected for sustained health and healing, it is not unreasonable to assume that when we feed "soul food" into our spirit, it is also beneficial to our physical body. Of course, I have no way to prove my hypothesis, but it sure makes sense to me that our physical nature can be charged with supernatural power resulting from our faith in God to achieve healing that is considered miraculous.

Since my "life Bible verse" for over 60 years is related to my heart, my heart had to have been fortified with substantial soul food to rejuvenate it when it was dead.

"Trust in the Lord with all thine heart and lean not unto thine own understanding...in all thy ways, acknowledge Him and He shall direct thy paths" (Proverbs 3:5-6 KJV).

When my children were just 3 and 4 years old, I wrote a song with the words of Proverbs 3:5-6. I often sang it to them after our nightly prayers and also would regularly sing it together with them during the day. I've also now taught that "heart tune" to my grandsons and am blessed with "Merry Heart Moments" (MHMs) whenever I hear them sing it. Our heart is the center of everything, so to trust in the Lord with all our heart is to trust Him in and through everything, including when it stops beating.

My heart had been spiritually fed from the Word of God since my earliest awareness of my Creator, and that had to have given me a stronger physical heart. Consequently, just a little of my heart fortified with the Word of God could/would be powerful enough to positively respond to the electrical shock of the double defibrillators. Little is *much* when God is in it. God lived in my little heart with great benefits spiritually and physically.

∞ ∞ ∞

In the evening of the day I died, Rachel and Gavin had returned home from South Florida. Although physically and emotionally exhausted, Rachel and Melody took time to carefully prepare an ICU support package for me of photos, wooden flowers (live ones were not allowed in the ICU), balloons, cards and delightful personal items to decorate my room. They knew it made my heart happy to be in colorful, bright surroundings with photos of those I love most. They knew that a happy heart is a healthy heart, so they did everything possible to ensure I was happy so my heart also would be.

For the rest of the day and night after I'd been revived, and all my days in the ICU, my daughters were devoted to being my Personal Life Support (PLS). They placed my phone on my pillow tuned into my favorite praise and worship stations. My daughters understood the importance music has always had to bless my days with inspiration and joy. Therefore, they understood the importance of music to bless my soul, spirit, and heart in the ICU.

There is healing power in music, so to be bathed in a concert of glorious praise and worship would generate more healing of my body than mere meds and machines were capable of. Heaven is filled with an atmosphere of music where there is no sickness nor disease, so I believe that heavenly music on earth is beneficial for our physical, mental and spiritual health on earth. The heavenly songs of healing, deliverance, power, victory, joy, love and the greatness of God were to fill my room in the ICU every minute of every day and night, to help extinguish any element – physical or spiritual – that would hinder or threaten my survival and recovery.

Melody and Rachel also tuned my room's TV to the Hallmark Channel™ since I'm a fan of seeing the stories in which relational and life problems conclude with "happily ever after." Even though it was on mute most of the time, just the images on the TV made me believe that the story of my life would be like one of those movies, not only with a happy ending but also with a happy beginning.

Melody and Rachel's presence and help in the ICU were essential for my recovery. I could not be fully restored to abundant life with only machines and the professional expertise of those assigned to poke needles into my neck, arms and ankles and inject mind altering, pain relieving, and health promising drugs into my system. PLS was necessary for HLS (Hospital Life Support) to work as GS (God Support) was designed to do. Everyone needs an advocate when in the hospital, and I was blessed with the best. PLS and GS, which all resulted in MLS and HLS (Mechanical Life and Hospital Life Support) to continue perpetuating the blessings of my heart miracle. It was like a new text message over and over: PLS + ML & HLS + GS = RAL & HM (Restored Abundant Life and Heart Miracle). OMG! LOL! TBIYTC!

Double defibs started my heart beating again, but now the double support and devotion of my twin daughters was ensuring the best for me. They were genuine double blessings, for through them God revealed His amazing Love. My DSD (Double Support Daughters) were dedicated to be as Heavenly light in the darkest of days. They were constantly stroking my swollen arms and speaking words of hope and encouragement. Also, since they'd witnessed such a phenomenal miracle, they were often laughing from an overflow of their joyful hearts in knowing that no matter what happens, God is in control. All that my daughters did to cultivate a spirit of Heaven in the ICU, in what I could see, feel and hear, was to ensure total healing of not just my body, but also of my mind and spirit.

Our physical bodies are ruled by our soul and spirit. Therefore, physical healing is often realized most in what we cannot see. Through the invisible sensing of beauty, laughter, love, faith and hope, little by little, one minute at a time, I was blessed with healing strength and rejuvenation.

My room faced a beautiful river with glorious skies dotted with "cotton candy colored clouds" and indescribably magnificent sunsets exploding with layers of a divine spectrum of purples, pinks, and golds. Although I could not consciously enjoy the spectacular view for days, nor retain the memory of all that I had witnessed, my eyes were consuming the blessings of the grand vistas declaring the Glory of God, and my body and spirit were absorbing the healing blessings of Heavenly beauty.

This was evident in how my daughters told me that I would gaze out the window with my eyes open and point out to them clouds that appeared as angels; laugh at dolphins jumping waves on the majestic river; delight in the slowly moving sparkling waters that seemed to be covered in diamonds; marvel at the deep blue skies and snow white puffy clouds, and be astonished at colors and artistry of the evening sky. Beauty is calming, beauty is healing. Whoever designed that heart hospital understood what is good for the heart. The large windows overlooking such glorious sights were healing for both patients and their caregivers in the ICU. It was the opposite of the depressing, dark and grey atmosphere of a basement ICU facility where I spent countless hours with my husband during his last years in this world. The view from my ICU room was as healing and good for my daughters as it was for me. Indeed, my eternal soul was reunited with my temporary physical body, and so far, even in the Intensive Care Unit, it was feeling good.

Chapter 5

I SAW ANGELS

"Even when walking through the dark valley of death I will not be afraid, for you are close beside me, guarding, guiding all the way" (Psalm 23:4).

"For he orders his angels to protect you wherever you go" (Psalm 91:11).

Just as I have no memory of even one minute of my life on April 23, 2022, I have no memory of the four days following when I was in the ICU, with the exception of an awareness of two companions alongside me on a journey through "outer space." I saw angels. Two glorious beings of light and peace accompanied me through darkness. They possessed a piercing brilliance and multi-dimensional luminescence with no distinguishable physical features. To look upon them was like gazing at the sun without hurting my eyes. The substance of their appearance was pure light in the form of men. They did not speak with audible sounds but seemed to communicate the message that "all is well." The silhouette of their presence was focused forward, as if they were watchers of what was ahead. Their purpose was to surround me with protection and assurance that I was not alone as I was flying through "the valley of death."

My daughters told me how, when I was "unconsciously conscious" in the ICU, I'd spoken of seeing angels. They asked me if they were good or bad angels. I responded with a smile that they were "good angels and so beautiful." I knew I had witnessed what God's Word tell us happens when we die. Angels really do take us on our journey to Heaven (Luke 16:22). It's no wonder most fear dying; it's truly a lonely process. Thoughts of drifting alone through darkness are frightening. So it's comforting to be assured that just as God has assigned angels to minister to us through our life on earth, they are also with us through the journey from this earth.

Nearly seven months after my 7-year-old grandson Carson witnessed my death, we talked again about what happened. I asked him what he was thinking when he was alone with me in the car while his Aummy Melody ran into the hospital for help. He said he felt "like he was flying into outer space." I can't help but wonder if Carson somehow knew that it was merely my physical body in the seat in front of him, and that the real me was on a celestial journey, soaring through the outer realms of darkness. It made me feel as if he wanted to be flying with me so I wouldn't be alone like he was while he sat in the hot car until Melody returned with help. I know that just as Heaven is for real, the presence of angels all around us is also real.

The morning I died is not the only time that I have witnessed the presence of angels; it has happened before.

∞ ∞ ∞

If we believe the Bible is true, then we know that just as God allowed angels to reveal themselves in scriptural accounts, He continues to do so. There certainly isn't any indication that God changed His mind about angel assignments:

> *"Therefore, angels are only servants—spirits sent to care for people who will inherit salvation"* (Hebrews 1:14).

Sometimes, we feel their presence with a brush of wind; sometimes we see cloud formations that our hearts interpret as actual manifestations of angels, and they very well could be; sometimes we actually can see them with mortal vision as beings of glorious light and beauty, and other times we know they have been near us in the form of man, or even perhaps birds, as when John baptized Jesus:

> *"After his baptism, as soon as Jesus came up out of the water, the heavens were opened to him and he saw the Spirit of God coming down in the form of a dove"* (Matthew 3:16).

While writing the concluding chapters of this book in early 2023, a bird perched on my windowsill at about 8AM every morning. I wondered if it was an angel sent to fill my heart with delight as a reminder of angels all around us as I worked on composing words of joy and hope for others.

My first awareness of a guardian angel was when I was only 3 years old. I was kidnapped – snatched from my tricycle in front of my house in Ohio – taken by a man who carried me into a dark garage (evil loves dark places). There he demanded I eat what looked to me then like "peas." He attempted to do the unthinkable. As he moved toward me, an unseen force firmly restrained him. Gazing at the ceiling with his mouth wide open in disbelief, his face turned white with fright. A bright and blinding light consumed the darkness. He screamed and ran away. I recall someone (an angel) guiding me back to the front door of my home. I walked into the living room where two policemen were talking with my parents. My mother had been crying hysterically, my father was anxious and pacing about, but when they saw me they both were crying and rejoicing.

Forty-four years later, just a few months before my mother died, she told me she thought she'd seen angels in her hospital room. I didn't doubt it was true and reminded her of when I'd been kidnapped. She was surprised to know that I'd remembered what had happened since I was so young when it did. I can understand why she did not talk about it with me through the years. It served no good purpose to dwell on such a traumatic incident. As such a young child then, no good would have come from learning what could have happened. It was enough to realize that I was safe because of the intervention of God. I believe my awareness of the supernatural as such a young child led to my acceptance of Jesus Christ into my life as Lord and Savior at age 4.

Once I started reading the Bible when I was about 7, my faith and understanding grew to the point that I knew God really does send angels when we pray, even if it's just short prayers such as, "Help, Lord," or calling out the name of Jesus.

At age 14, I was again to see what I knew to be true about angelic protection. I was volunteering to work in the office of my junior high and was dispatched to pick up books from the school library. As I walked past the stairway leading to the front entrance of the school building, I looked out the window to see a huge mob headed toward the doors. In moments, they burst through the doors. I froze, wondering what was happening.

A large group from the mob surrounded me, knocked the books out of my hands, pulled my hair, pushed me to the floor, squirted me with water guns, and some flipped knives threatening me while shouting, "Black Power." I really did not know what they meant. I grew up in a neighborhood where kids were just kids; we did not think of each other as kids of one color or kids of another color, any more than we thought of some people as short or others as tall. There were those we would sometimes refer to as bad and good people, but it wasn't because of the way they looked, it was because of what they did or did not do.

While lying on the cold, hard hallway floor, I was in shock and speechless. I lifted my head up slowly and used all my strength to cry out, "Jesus!" Just recalling what happened next still gives me chills. A light shone in that dark hallway. The expressions of those determined to do harm transformed from hatred to fear, much like what I'd remembered seeing on the face of the kidnapper when alone in a dark, wet, dreary garage eleven years before. The attackers stopped, paralyzed in fear; their only movement was to place knives in their pockets and slowly back away from me, creating a way to for me to escape. Their stone-cold faces were unable to shout threats, nor speak even a word as I felt a gentle spirit helping me stand and guiding me through the now quiet mob. As I walked lightly past the now silent attackers, no one could touch me, pull my hair, or even attempt to block my pathway to safety.

Leaving the books that were scattered and stepped on, all eyes were on me, but they said nothing. While entering the open passage created for me to safely leave the center of turmoil, I felt as if I were supernaturally transported safely to the principal's office where I found refuge with others who'd gone there for protection. Many were harmed that day. I heard that a teenage boy had died from a similar mob attack at the nearby high school.

Through the simple prayer, "Jesus," God revealed those guardian angels to my attackers just as He'd done for Elisha on the battlefield when surrounded by mobs of enemy soldiers.

> *"So one night the king of Syria sent a great army with many chariots and horses to surround the city. When the prophet's servant got up early the next morning and went outside, there were troops, horses, and chariots everywhere. 'Alas, my master, what shall we do now?' he cried out to Elisha. 'Don't be afraid!' Elisha told him. 'For our army is bigger than theirs!' Then Elisha prayed, 'Lord, open his eyes and let him see!' And the Lord opened the young man's eyes so that he could see horses of fire and chariots of fire everywhere upon the mountain!"* (II Kings 6:17-20).

God opened the eyes of Elisha and those fighting with him in the midst of that overwhelming battle to experience the reality of the spiritual dimension. He saw warrior angels in charge of horses and chariots of fire surrounding him. I only saw the light of an angelic presence on the day of the attack against me as a teenager, but I sure do believe my attackers' eyes were opened to see warrior angels. What is *unseen* in the spiritual realm is truly what controls our lives far more than we realize.

Twice I've been riding in vans when angels intervened to save my family. The first incident was when my son was only about 4 years old and the twins were 3, during the years my husband and I traveled as full-time music evangelists. Since we often served in remote churches where the need was greatest, the journey to them could be dangerous and difficult. It was particularly challenging to navigate through narrow mountain roads in Western Colorado.

One sunny day, we were traveling on such a challenging road when a truck was suddenly coming directly toward us. There was no way we could avoid a head-on collision. On our left was the side of the mountain and on the right a steep cliff. Just before a most certain impact, there was flash of light and we found ourselves in a grassy meadow. For a few minutes, my husband and I were still in disbelief.

People approached our van to check on us. They had witnessed what had no natural explanation. Our van had been supernaturally transported to safety. As the people confirmed that what had happened was the intervention of a guardian angel, we both simultaneously shouted, "Hallelujah," and gave praise and thanks to God. We kept singing praises of thanksgiving to God all the way to our destination. We were also vividly reminded of the importance of always praying for safe travels!

When my daughters were teenagers, we were riding back from one of their junior tennis tournaments in our mini-van between Wichita Falls and Fort Worth, Texas with our snow white American Eskimo dog named Angel. Suddenly, a tornado lifted our van off the highway. It was dark so we couldn't see anything; there was just the feeling of flying round and round. My husband was at the wheel and I was sitting in the front seat. Melody and Rachel held Angel tightly in the back seat. Our natural response was to pray over and over: "Jesus, help us!"

Momentarily, our van came to rest on the opposite side of the highway and we could see the headlights of cars coming toward us. We kept shouting, "Jesus, Jesus, Jesus, Jesus, protect us. Help us!" Again, we felt a powerful thrust of wind lift up our van, twirl us around, and set us down. We emerged to see we were on the shoulder of the highway facing the right direction. Other people walked over to check if we were okay, for they couldn't believe what they'd just seen. As the twirling winds sucked us into the midst of that intense storm, the lights of our van had made us visible to everyone who'd sought shelter under a nearby bridge. We had no doubt that our cries had reached Jesus, who dispatched angels to carry us to safety.

I felt that both my parents were seeing angels just before they died and were pointing and talking about seeing what others around us could not see. When I was with my father (I called him Pa) late on the night before he died, I sat beside his bed singing old hymns from his favorite hymnal. I was grieved by not being able to understand why God would allow such pain and suffering, especially for anyone who truly loved the Lord. I was overcome with sorrow at not being able to make sense of it all. I found solace through the lyrics of old hymns written by those who had been through hardship and heartache and experienced the prevailing power of God in and through it all.

I wasn't sure whether my father could hear me as he lay motionless in a coma, but I was hoping and praying that perhaps singing familiar hymns would bring him comfort as it did for me. He had directed choirs and led in hymn singing worship for many years in churches on Sundays and for Wednesday night prayer meetings for as long as I could remember. Hymns were a regular part of his life.

I began my "serenade of hope" to him with a tune I'd been singing since boarding the plane from Texas to Ohio to be by his side:

> This world is not my home, I'm just a'passin through,
> my treasures are laid up, somewhere beyond the blue;
> the angels beckon me through Heaven's open doors,
> and I can't feel at home in this world anymore....
>
> (Jim Reeves, 1923-1964)

I continued singing and weeping for hours while praying the songs would be comforting to my Pa. He remained unresponsive. I was discouraged that he might not even be able to hear me. Emotionally and physically exhausted and missing my young children, I decided it was time to leave. but before going to sing Daniel, Melody and Rachel to sleep, I was compelled to sing just one more of Pa's most favorite hymns. Opening the old hymnal to a random selection, my eyes rested on the page with one of Pa's favorites: *It Will Be Worth It All When We See Jesus©* (Esther Kerr Rosthoi, 1909-1962). As I sang, I wept even more. The words reminded me that this world is not our home, that one day everything that did not make sense will be understood.

51

Oft times the day seems long, our sorrows hard to bear;
we're tempted to complain, to murmur and despair.
But Christ will soon appear, to catch his bride away.
All tears will all be over in God's eternal day!

To my shock and in awe, I watched as Pa opened his eyes and joined me in singing the chorus:

It will be worth it all when we see Jesus,
Life trials will seem so small when we see Him.
One glimpse of His dear face, all sorrow will erase,
so bravely run the race, till we see Christ!

He then saw something I could not see. "What's that?" he asked. And just hours later, he was gone.

While my husband was in the ICU during his last days on earth, I'd brought a boom box to play cassette albums of songs we'd recorded and performed together in gospel concerts. We shared a mutual love and appreciation of the blessings of inspirational music. During the six years he battled bone cancer, we'd often sung together in his hospital rooms and doctors' offices. While we could no longer sing together, I knew he could hear the melodies that would prepare his heart – and those there with him – for his imminent departure.

Doctors and nurses were surprised that he did not die immediately after removing life support. It was evident to me he was not yet ready to go. Perhaps God would bring him back? As the recordings of our inspirational duets kept playing, he kept breathing. Nurses came in to see if monitors were operational; he wasn't supposed to still be alive without life support. But he stayed with us through song after song, listening to melodies declaring the promises of God's enduring presence, unlimited power, and steadfast love. He could not speak, but it seemed as if he was speaking to us through the music. Our recorded voices were transforming the atmosphere in that dreary ICU into an oasis of love, joy, hope and peace.

He continued to breathe and remained with us long after life support was removed. There was one more song yet to be played on our cassette album, and we wept when hearing this man who could no longer even speak beautifully singing:

When peace like a river, attendeth my way, when sorrows
like sea billows roll

Whatever my lot, thou hast taught me to say,
It is well with my soul:
Tho satan should buffet, though trials should come,
Let this blest assurance control;
That Christ hath regarded my helpless estate,
And hath shed His own blood for my soul;
My sin, oh the bliss of this glorious thought--
My sin, not in part, but in whole,
Is nailed to the cross and I bear it no more,
Praise the Lord, Praise the Lord, Oh My Soul!
Oh Lord haste the day when my faith shall be sight!
The clouds be rolled back as a scroll.
The trump shall resound and the Lord shall descend
Even so, it is well, it is well with my soul......

(*When Peace Like a River*© Horatio Gates Spafford, 1873)

Then, as our recorded voices together were singing the final notes: "It is well, with my soul. It is well, it is well. It is well with my soul," suddenly, my son Daniel, who'd been lying beside his dad, looked up at the ceiling and shouted the two words I'd heard my dad say just before he went Home, 'What's that?' At the moment the last sounds of *It is well with my soul* faded away, a holographic brilliance flowed down from above; a gentle wind that felt like being brushed by feathers swept hair across my face. My husband's soul then departed with the angels. I fell on my knees in tears and looked upwards as if I felt him looking down at me. He had no material wealth to leave behind, but he left us with a treasure far greater: A legacy of faith in knowing the reality of salvation through Jesus Christ as our Lord and Savior. He was gone, but not dead.

"For God so loved the world, that he gave his only begotten Son, that whosoever believeth in him should not perish, but have everlasting life" (John 3:16 KJV).

The experience was so unreal that I wondered if we had really seen what we saw.

Two weeks later, I was driving my car and pondering if I'd actually seen angels when my husband died. Emotionally overcome with grief and uncontrollable weeping, I pulled in to park in a safe place where I could pray. God filled my heart with comforting peace. I turned on the radio to listen to music until I felt it safe to drive. Instead of worship music, the station was broadcasting a message by David Jeremiah about angels at the time of death. My heart was consoled and blessed to hear how he and others had witnessed the presence of angels many times at the deaths of believers.

I've never since doubted the reality of angels all around us in life and in death. Another unforgettable angelic intervention occurred exactly one week after my husband's funeral when my house caught fire. My next-door neighbor had been shopping nearby and felt something urging her to leave the store and go home immediately. Driving toward our adjacent homes, she saw flames creeping along my roof. "Your house is on fire," she screamed, banging on my front door.

Her screams woke me from a deep sleep. I responded with shouts of, "Jesus!" over and over, while quickly grabbing my American Eskimo doggy, Angel, a few precious family photos, and original paintings of my deceased husband. Standing outside in the cold, with light snowflakes falling softly on me and disappearing slowly in the white fur of Angel, I noticed that her legs, back, and fluffy tail were covered with black soot. Time seemed to stand still, yet it only took mere moments for firetrucks to crowd the street of our home on Pennsylvania Avenue in Arlington, Texas.

My neighbor wasn't the only one to whom God had sent angels to warn us and to help keep Angel and me from harm. The city fire chief just happened to be driving nearby when he saw my roof engulfed in flames and he called for immediate help. I sat in the fire chief's truck with Angel on my lap, caressing her and saying over and over, "Jesus, Jesus, Jesus!" After about 20 minutes, the fire chief opened my door and told me I was "the luckiest woman alive!"

"What?"

"Your roof was totally destroyed!"

"What?"

"When a roof is destroyed, the house is always a total loss," he said.

"Mine isn't?"

"That's why you're the luckiest woman alive. Something happened I sure can't explain. The fire just stopped after the roof was destroyed."

He took me inside my now flooded home and flashed his light around the ceilings of each room on the second floor, revealing a near perfect separation between what had burned and what had not. Fire had miraculously stopped throughout the entire circumference of my home. Water and smoke filled the house, but fire had only consumed the roof. Before I knew about the fire, God had already responded to my need for help; guardian angels were ready to serve, even when I was sleeping and unaware my house was in flames. With my simple prayers of, "Jesus, Jesus, Jesus," the destructive force of the fire had come to a halt.

Before my husband's death, my son battled a deadly meth addiction which continued for nearly five years after he'd promised his dad (when lying beside him on his death bed) he would "never take drugs again." The story of his deliverance is a testimony of Divine angelic intervention to overcome the impossible.

I had served as a corporate chaplain for many years, regularly helping parents through times of crisis with their teenagers in bondage to drugs, but everything I'd done to help my own son had failed. During my husband's perpetual hospitalizations and throughout the years following his death, I was alone in an unceasing and exhausting struggle and battle to save my son's life. Even though I was physically alone, it became evident that God sustained us in ways I could not see. Securing the usual help for my addicted teenage son was never enough. Through unceasing prayers and persistent faith that God would make a way when their seemed to be no way, Daniel's ultimate deliverance would be initiated through an intervention arranged by a television production crew. It was originally broadcast nationally and internationally on A & E® Network's *Intervention*© in 2006 and rebroadcast for many years after.

During the years when I'd been passionately and fervently crying out for God to deliver, heal and restore Daniel's life, he told me that he'd often seen angels over me, coming through the ceiling and surrounding me. Daniel also told me of how his eyes were open to the reality of spiritual warfare, including in and around our house. He was able to see the battles in another dimension. Once, when he was nearly dead after receiving a tattoo and overdosing on meth, he'd seen a vision of the grandstands of Heaven where everyone shouted for him to "stay the course."

Witnessing angels intervene in my own personal life, and now in my death, has caused me to try to view what happens each day, and my responses, more through Heaven's eyes. Just as the Bible is full of healing miracles and resurrection miracles, there are mentions throughout God's Word about the ministry of angels. One of my favorites that I read and weave into my daily prayers for myself and my family is worth repeating again here:

"For he orders his angels to protect you wherever you go.
They will steady you with their hands to keep you from stumbling against the rocks on the trail" (Psalm 91:11-12).

Angels are a reassuring presence to help us to not die before God's work in and through us is complete. Remembering the angels with me at death helps me now to never doubt their protective help on earth. From earth's perspective I may seem to be alone, but God ensures that I never am.

I did not witness "angels of death" but "angels of life" who had been with me all the days of my life. The memory of those angels who were with me as I traveled through "the valley of the shadow of death" gives me the hope that God will absolutely fulfill Gavin's prophecy over me when he declared that God was not finished with me yet. God has assured me that I have not yet fulfilled my ordained destiny and mission on earth. I am to take Gavin's words to heart every day – one day at a time – for what he declared is a promise from God's Word:

"And I am sure that God who began the good work within you will keep right on helping you grow in his grace until his task within you is finally finished on that day when Jesus Christ returns" (Philippians 1:6).

My heart is strengthened in knowing that warrior angels have always, and continue to, protect me and my family through our earthly battles to prevent the attacks of the enemy to kill, steal and destroy. With angels all around me, I joyfully continue the good fight of faith.

There is nothing like dying and coming back to life again to renew hope and faith in God's Word and purpose for living.

"No, dear brothers, I am still not all I should be, but I am bringing all my energies to bear on this one thing: Forgetting the past and looking forward to what lies ahead, I strain to reach the end of the race and receive the prize for which God is calling us up to heaven because of what Christ Jesus did for us" (Philippians 3:13-14).

∞ ∞ ∞

Witnessing the shining presence of angels flying with me through eternity, lighting the way and piercing the darkness of the spiritual domain, has reminded me that God will not only light our way in this dark world, but we are to shine as lights of hope.

"Jesus said to the people, 'I am the Light of the world. So if you follow me, you won't be stumbling through the darkness, for living light will flood your path'" (John 8:12).

"Don't hide your light! Let it shine for all; let your good deeds glow for all to see" (Matthew 5:16).

The light from the angels I saw when I was in the darkness of death, and the light from the angels I witnessed during dark days throughout my life, is the same light that shines through us in this dark world for others to see Jesus wherever we are.

Jesus said in John 14:6 that He is *"the Way, the Truth and the Life."* In John 8:12, as just stated, we are reminded that He lights the way to abundant life on earth and eternal life in Heaven: *"Jesus said to the people, 'I am the Light of the world. So if you follow me, you won't be stumbling through the darkness, for living light will flood your path.'"* The closer we are to our Creator, the more we are going to *"shine"* from the light of His spirit within our hearts.

There is a constant battle between darkness and light in this world. But with the light of *Jesus* in our hearts shining bright and the light of *angels* serving and helping us in and through all things, we can rejoice in knowing that in the battle between darkness and light, light always wins.

> ### This Little Light of Mine (traditional)
> "This little light of mine, I'm gonna let it shine.
> This little light of mine, I'm gonna let it shine
> This little light of mine, I'm gonna let it shine,
> let it shine, let it shine let it shine.
> Let it shine till Jesus comes,
> won't let satan blow it out
> I'm gonna let it shine, let it shine, let it shine.
> Let it shine 'til Jesus comes, let it shine, let it shine, let it shine."

God's will for us is not a mystery at all. We are to SHINE.

You don't need to die and come back to life or see angels like I did to truly live until you die. You just need to SHINE.

You don't have to see Heaven or see angels to be blessed with the blessings of Heaven and angels, for the Bible says: "*.... blessed are those who have* **not seen** *and yet* **have believed**" (John 20:29, emphasis added).

Chapter 6

A WALKING MIRACLE

"I am the Lord, The GOD of all mankind. Is anything too hard for me?"
(Jeremiah 32:7)
"He performs wonders that cannot be fathomed. ...miracles that cannot be counted"
(Job 5:9).
"God did extraordinary miracles through Paul "(Acts 19:11).
"What is impossible with man, is possible with God" (Luke 18:27 NIV).
"Now glory be to God, who by his mighty power at work within us is able to do far more than we would ever dare to ask or even dream of—infinitely beyond our highest prayers, desires, thoughts, or hopes" (Ephesians 3:20).

Where am I?

Five days after I had died, I opened my eyes to be fully conscious of not being at home. *Where was Karly? Had something happened to Karly? I need to see Karly! She had fallen asleep beside me and should be licking my face, wagging her tail and anxious for our morning walk.*

I had closed my eyes on a Friday night with my sweet Karly's head resting on my ankle, and consciously opened them five days later in an environment that I recognized as a hospital room that was strangely familiar. I had no understanding of why I was in a hospital.

As I said, my left arm was swollen twice its normal size. Irritating and uncomfortable IV's were in my neck and arms. When seeing an identification bracelet on my ankle, I thought, *isn't that where they put identification for a dead person?*

"Do you remember me?" a kind and familiar stranger asked, smiling when entering my room as if he fully expected me to actually know him.

59

The brightness of the sun shining through the window temporarily blinded my ability to distinguish the features of this man I did not know, but who knew me.

"I was with you in the room when you came back to life."

What? Come back to life? I was dead?

"You are a walking miracle?"

How? Why?

This was no stranger; he was a doctor with me when I was dead and who had witnessed the miracle of my resurrection. Although I did not consciously recognize this wonderful doctor, my heart was filled with gratitude for him as if I had known him from somewhere.

"Thank you so very much. God bless you," was my natural whisper-voice response for his encouraging presence.

The doctor said, "God has a plan for what He did through you; you need to tell everyone; you must write a book. Your testimony gives hope."

Hope?

I did not fully understand how or why, but something in my heart was in total agreement with all that he said. He then prayed with and for me. When he left, I thought of how every life is a genuine miracle. Just being able to walk and talk, dance and sing, eat and sleep, love and cry, breathe and run, create and procreate, is truly miraculous.

Think about what fuels all of the above. It is a muscle the size of our fist, beating 100,000 times every single day, pumping five or six quarts of blood each minute, 2000 quarts a day, is miraculous.

But we are so accustomed to taking for granted the miracle of just being alive, that for something to be considered a genuine, absolute, definite miracle has to be an occurrence that no one can logically, scientifically or even philosophically attempt to explain; it must be an extremely rare impossible occurrence.

A miracle transcends all possibilities. Everyone is fascinated with stories of miracles. Miracles are only possible through the power of our Creator. Therefore, when we hear of miracles, it draws us closer to knowing God.

We refer to those involved in a miracle as themselves being a miracle. Not because of their own supernatural power, but because of what the "Miracle Maker" has done in and through them. The character of God is manifested through the ordinary miracles of all of life that we often take for granted, such as the miracle of a beating heart. However, it is the miracles beyond the ordinary that inspire magnified hope within the miraculous beat of every heart.

I believe that is why, in our chaotic and often scary world, God is revealing His power and presence to encourage us to know that no matter what happens, He is in control. Miracles remind us of God's omnipotent, steadfast power to overcome and be victorious in and through all things. That is why I believe that as wars and chaos escalate, we are witnessing more miraculous events than ever before. In realizing the power of the supernatural to overcome the natural, hope grows in our seemingly hopeless world. God performs miracles so that we will see and know, without a doubt, that His Word is true; that He understands what we are going through; that He knows us and cares about us, and that He is always with us to help us conquer the challenges, the pain, the overwhelming concerns in this fallen world.

When surrounded by a culture of hopelessness, an extraordinary miracle reminds us that no matter what happens, *nothing* is too difficult for God as we put our trust in Him. Nothing in this world can give us real and lasting hope. Hope is not natural, it is supernatural. This world is temporary. God is eternal.

Miracles are a gift of hope from our loving Savior to help us know we rest in His Hands. His joy in our hearts is our strength to save and help us in every situation. Miracles assure us God's promises are not limited to those we think are most deserving. It doesn't matter how old, young, rich, or poor, because anyone from anywhere in any situation who chooses to put their trust in the Lord instead of what is in this world, can and often does, experience a miracle.

But God gives us the choice. We have a choice to trust in God with a heart of joy and faith, or for our hearts to be filled with anxiety and fear. When we trust in the things of this world and are tempted by the god of this world to pursue only what this world offers, we cannot realize the blessings of being a "walking miracle" with a "heart of joy and hope." When we trust in Jesus, we are assured of His power within us to live victoriously until we die. If we trust only in what this fallen world offers, we are tempted to die before we are dead.

Miracles remind us that what is not seen is the true reality. And through miracles we are reminded that what we do not see controls what we can see. It is the spiritual world that determines and controls all that happens in the physical world.

> *"By faith—by believing God—we know that the world and the stars—in fact, all things—were made at God's command; and that they were all made from things that can't be seen"* (Hebrews 11:3).

What we see with our physical eyes is not all there is, and what we are able to see with earthly eyes is temporary and imperfect. It can be rightly concluded that what we do not see now is the true reality. We live in a temporary world with only a minute understanding of the eternal.

> *"... we can see and understand only a little about God now, as if we were peering at his reflection in a poor mirror; but someday we are going to see Him in his completeness, face-to-face. Now all that I know is hazy and blurred, but then I will see everything clearly, just as clearly as God sees into my heart right now"* (I Corinthians 13:1).

Miracles remind us that man cannot save you, but God can. Man cannot do the impossible, but God can. Miracles help teach us to trust in what we cannot see to help us through what we can see.

In all of life, miracles remind us of whom we trust with all our hearts.

> *"It is better to trust the Lord than to put confidence in men. It is better to take refuge in Him than in the mightiest king!"* (Psalm 118:8-9)

All praise and glory is only to God in the midst of a miracle!

A miracle can draw someone close to God who may never have believed in God, and can open their eyes of understanding to trust in Jesus Christ as their personal Lord and Savior. A miracle touches the hearts of those who already know the Lord to be encouraged and inspired and strengthened in their faith and purpose knowing, without a doubt, that God has not forgotten them. Miracles assure us, "God's got this!"

Miracles can make it seem as if Heaven has come to earth. In so doing, we are reminded more to pray God's will be done on earth as it is in Heaven. The greater the need of a miracle, the greater our joy when they happen.

Miracles do inspire hope...

My personal heart miracle of 2022 has pierced my understanding of Psalm 34:18 as never before: *"The Lord is close to the brokenhearted and saves those who are crushed in spirit."*

My heart had broken physically and spiritually, but when I was heartbroken, the presence of God enveloped my soul with a closer awareness of His love, and a renewed hope of a blessed and purposeful future.

Since God is the substance of every miracle, any person who is blessed by a miracle assuredly is drawn closer to our Lord and Savior. Even those who do not know the Lord experience a sense of knowing in their hearts that there is a higher power at work in the midst of the miraculous.

All the miracles I have heard of – and especially the most major and profound one I have experienced – have one consistent element: **Prayer.**

It is beyond my ability to fully comprehend with finite human understanding how or why God has chosen flawed humans to accomplish His perfect will through prayer. I just know He does! The substance of prayer is faith:

> *"And without faith it is impossible to please God"* (Hebrews 11:16).

Prayer is the key to Heaven, but faith unlocks the door to the miraculous. I know, without a doubt, miracles happen when we pray that will not happen if we do not pray. The more prayer, the more power to overcome the impossible.

I could not have become a "walking miracle" if no one prayed for me when I could not pray for myself.

As I'm writing this book, there is news of a professional football player, Damar Hamlin, who momentarily died from sudden cardiac arrest in the middle of a televised game on January 3, 2023. Immediately, thousands and perhaps millions prayed for him. He, too, experienced a miracle and came back to life. But you don't have to be a star athlete with a team of medical professionals ready to respond through prayers for God to do the miraculous. God can use a young woman driving a car when her mom dies beside her, or send a few Holy Spirit-filled doctors to be just where they were needed to reveal His miraculous power through prayer. God uses people and things everywhere and anywhere when we need a miracle.

My walking miracle is proof that prayers are never in vain. Prayers are not just words, but faith in action. Miracles can – and very often do – happen when you pray for your family, friends, strangers, your neighborhood, your city, state and nation. Absolutely anything and everything can be positively influenced and helped through prayer.

When someone asks you to pray, when you hear of or witness someone in need – even when you have just a thought to pray – then pray. Don't worry about the outcome, for when you pray, God's will is done. When my grandsons were little, they would often initiate prayers for those in ambulances passing by us or those involved in automobile accidents we witnessed.

Just as the seemingly simple prayer of, "Help, Lord," can bring Jesus' power into any dilemma, so it will when we are praying for strangers.

Don't be discouraged because prayers haven't always seemed to be answered as we would like them to be. To pray is a spiritual battle in which we cannot see or know everything that is happening. In Daniel 10:13, you can read the story of how Daniel's prayers were hindered by the Prince of Persia, but he kept praying.

The greater the purpose for our prayers, the greater the battles will be. That is why we cannot give up, why we must keep praying even when we do not feel like it. We must understand that answers to our prayers can be immediate, but our petitions may take days, weeks, months and years to be fulfilled.

Although we cannot expect all of what we consider the best outcomes when we pray, we can be assured as we pray that somehow, someway, all things will work together for good for those who love the Lord. When we pray, we have peace in knowing that we can't always yet see the "why" our prayers are not yet answered, but we know that if we do not pray, then we can miss out on God's best.

Every day as I feel my heart beating, I am reminded to invite God's intervention through prayer into every concern of each day. My big miracle has given me confidence that even little miracles should be a regular part of our daily lives.

One way this became evident was when I started to drive again after my big miracle and my car was constantly "dying."

Each time I would pray for it to start, yet it would have to be towed again to repair shops where mechanics could never determine why it was constantly malfunctioning.

After exhausting my resources paying for multiple repairs that resulted in only temporary fixes, I needed to engage in more determined warfare prayer. So, when I stood by my broken-down car on the side of the road while a mechanic had failed in numerous attempts to jump start it to avoid towing it again for fruitless repairs, I shouted, "Father God, bring my car back to life just as you did my heart, in Jesus' name. Amen!" The mechanic who initially thought I was acting rather strangely, was shocked that he was able to start the car immediately after that prayer. It was at least several months later that my car broke down again.

∞∞∞∞

Before the kind doctor left and again after we prayed, he told me to start writing a book as soon as possible, reminding me again of how my testimony of hope was needed in our world more than ever.

Even though I had yet to learn of the extent of my heart miracle, his words pierced my heart and confirmed his wise counsel was not to be taken lightly.

When the doctor prayed, and when others came into my room who also prayed with me, I felt my damaged heart begin to heal. Little by little, Jesus was indeed changing me. I would never be the same person I used to be.

I prayed for everyone God sent into my room. My prayers were for God to give them favor, wisdom, and strength to be all He created them to be. I encouraged them to realize that they, like me, were also walking miracles ordained by God to live with hearts of joy.

Chapter 7

GOD BLESS YOU IN THE ICU

"The Lord bless you and keep you; the Lord make his face shine on you and be gracious to you; the Lord turn his face toward you and give you peace"' (Numbers 6:24-26).

"**G**od bless you," I whispered.

The nurses had just removed the breathing tube which had been inserted three days earlier down through my mouth, throat, vocal chords and windpipe. Since I'd received the emergency intubation, I was at particular risk for damage that could lead to difficulty swallowing and speaking for weeks, or even months, and most definitely at risk for needing speech therapy.

The breathing tube had been part of my life support to keep me from dying again, but what made the difference in my recovery was not just the mechanical and medicinal life support, but the implementation of GS (God Support). This is the supernatural rejuvenation of dead and damaged cells within every part of me, because GS perpetually infused my physical body with restorative power. GS was (and is) activated through unceasing prayers, praise and worship to Jehovah Rapha (God who heals) in the name of Jesus. Part of what activates GS is a thankful heart. A thankful heart is one filled with gratitude. A grateful heart is one that seeks to bless others.

During those days, I was in a "consciously unconscious" state, attempting to communicate, but not aware of doing so. Because of damage from the tube that had just been removed, I could only speak in soft whispers, but from what I was told, my whispers in the ICU were filled with, "God bless yous." Even while unconscious, my heart was aware of how God had blessed me and evidently my desire was to bless others as I had been so greatly blessed. Therefore, "God bless you" would be my soft greeting to anyone and everyone who entered and departed from my room in the ICU. If I could not say anything else, I wanted to at least say, "God bless you."

Powerful drugs affected my cognitive awareness in much the same way as those who have consumed too much alcohol and say whatever is on their minds. I was conversing but was not consciously aware of anything I was saying. What I spoke was what I was unconsciously thinking in that moment.

The person who becomes talkative when drunk with alcohol wakes up the next day not remembering anything once the poison flushes out of their system. I was constantly being injected with substances to manage pain and assist healing, substances that were to perpetually keep me in a talkative state of appearing to be conscious. These medications would, however, prevent me from remembering anything I said or did, not for just one day, but for nearly five days. Just like a person who awakens after a drunken stupor hopes they didn't say or do anything they'd regret, I hoped the same for myself when learning of my talkative unconscious state.

It's amazing and perplexing to me to learn that during my drug induced mental state I was not only alert, but I also was anxious to communicate. Even though I could only whisper, I still wanted to vocalize fascinating stories about my life and observations from my ICU confinement.

Over and over, as both strangers and family would wander in my room, I would whisper, "God bless you," when they entered, for as long as they were with me, and as they were leaving. My voice was weak and raspy, but my determination was strong and clear to use my voice to impart God's blessings to all who cared about me and for me. There is power in words. As I had experienced the ultimate power promised in the Word of God in every cell of my being, I wanted His power of blessing to fall upon everyone.

While lying peacefully in the ICU, my mind and heart were perpetually absorbing the sounds of the beauty and the truth of God's faithfulness, goodness, love and healing through those around me, and through heavenly music. As the glorious sounds permeated the atmosphere, life was being restored to my broken body, minute by minute, day by day.

Even in my "consciously unconscious" state of being, it was as if the celestial music filled my heart with a perpetual desire to bless others as I had been so greatly blessed. I could not do much of anything, but I could speak a prayerful blessing upon all those God brought to me while I was incapacitated. Even if my chest hurt when I tried to whisper and it would often make me cough, I was unceasingly motivated to whisper as much as I could; something within my heart was moved to say over and over, "God bless you."

I had learned the importance of blessings years ago when fighting for the lives of my husband and son. During those years which seemed as "hell on earth," I learned that while we cannot always be blessed, we can be a blessing. It became evident that we are most greatly blessed when we are a blessing to others. Even in the worst of the worst life of "not blessed," there can still be a way to be a blessing. So, even in the ICU when I was powerless to do much of anything, I could still at least whisper, "God bless you." Whether unconsciously or consciously, every time I did, my heart was blessed.

Years ago, I began making positive declarations into what I refer to as "Joyisms" that are catchy phrases to remind me of how to maintain a joyful heart, even in the midst of situations that were not joy filled. My first "Joyism" was: "The best is yet to come" (TBIYTC). My second "Joyism" was: "To be blessed, be a blessing" (TBBBAB). These and other "Joyisms," such as "Don't Sweat the Small Stuff" (DSTSS), inspire me to pray for God's will to be done on earth as it is in Heaven and to live each day from an eternal perspective. My "Joyisms" also encourage me to discover ways to be blessed with a heart of joy even when in situations not considered "blessed." It's beneficial for everyone to create their own unique "Joyisms" as reminders to live our lives through Heaven's eyes.

Musical blessings were also an important part of my ICU recovery. Music has always been a vital part of my life, so much so that I named my first daughter Melody Joy. How appropriate that my daughter, whose name means "song of joy," would be used to save my life and ensure I was unceasingly blessed in an atmosphere of perpetual songs of joy during that most intensely critical time of my life. And how amazing that my daughter Rachel, whose name means "lamb of God," would also help create a rejuvenating musical ambiance in the hospital room, reminding me of the Lamb of God's healing presence and power for such a time as this.

Ecclesiastes 4:9 tells us "*...two are better than one...*" and as the mom of twins this has always had a very special meaning. At no time previously was there a more profound and demonstrative proof of "two being better than one" than when my twins excelled far better together than either could have alone during those critical days when double blessings were greatly needed in the ICU.

The positive and beautiful musical environment of healing they created, coupled with their doubly good encouraging words, attentive kindness, and faithful support, did far more than meds and machines, or what the very best doctors and nurses could ever possibly accomplish alone.

Intermixed between the "God bless yous" in the ICU, in an atmosphere of healing melodies, my unconsciously conscious conversations were also humorous and enlightening. I conversed about things I was not even thinking about when conscious, and some things that happened decades ago.

Again, I can't help but compare my drugged mind and body to those who've consumed too much alcohol that results in focusing on concerns that normally would not be considered important, and/or things we would not even normally want to talk about at all. Powerful drugs flowing through my system had the same effect. As I said before, unlike someone who eventually awakens with conscious awareness after the alcohol has left their system, my system did not have a break from the drugs that were keeping me in a perpetual state of conscious unconsciousness.

So, my unusual conversations went on for days. Some were a result of my faulty perception of where I was or why I was there, such as saying I was in Ohio where I was born and grew up, rather than in a hospital in Jacksonville, Florida. Mind-altering drugs may help relieve pain and help with healing, but it is rather scary to realize their potentially strange effects on the brain. People in the hospital sometimes might appear delusional, but it could merely be a consequence of pain medications on cerebral activity.

I've been a singer all my life, so it wasn't surprising to learn I was not just "whisper-talking" but also was "whisper-singing" when I was unconsciously conscious. Out of the thousands of melodies I've committed to memory during the past 66 years, what I chose to sing was rather comical. There were tunes I started whisper-singing that I hadn't thought about for decades, such as one I'd sung to my children when they were babies. The lyrics of this simple melody, composed by my babies' daddy, seemed to be my subconsciously conscious way of explaining all that was going on:

> Little by little every day, little by little in every way, Jesus is changing me.

He's changing me, my blessed Savior,
I'm not the same person that I used to be.

It's been slow going, but there's a knowin' that
one day perfect I will be…

This simple song was simply profound. God sure was changing me. There is no way I will ever be the same person again.

In my unconscious consciousness, it seemed as if deep in my soul I embraced the blessed assurance of knowing God was still working on me, changing me to be and become all He ordained for my life before I was to leave my physical body for good. I felt as if I was unknowingly given "hope pills" not just for healing, but also for hope in the changes I needed to continue to undergo to become all God created me for.

We've all heard someone say that what goes in, comes out, meaning whatever we consume into our minds will come out through what we say and do. If we consume thoughts of joy and love, we generally are more joyful and loving. If we put mayhem and misery into our minds, we tend to be disruptive and miserable. If we put what is edifying, profound and significant into our minds, we usually tend to speak with more inspirational wisdom.

In Proverbs 23:7 we read, *"As a man thinks in his heart, so is he."* This verse has new meaning now to me; what was coming out of me in words and music was what I had put into me through thoughts and music. We should all realize that what we're choosing to consume mentally remains in our minds. Our brains are amazing, intricate, organic systems storing the memories of all our lives. Just think of what might come out of your mind if you are drugged up in a hospital for just one day. It's funny what we sometimes blurt out when we are conscious of what we're saying, but what we might speak while unconscious can be even more hilarious.

All our life experiences remain in our unconscious mind, so even when we think we have put the past past, and never consciously think or talk about unpleasant memories, they are never completely erased. Therefore, when our brains have been infused with mind altering drugs, those memories can "escape" from cells of unconsciousness into semi-conscious conversations. I was to learn how embarrassingly true this was during one day in the ICU when I whispered to Rachel for no apparent reason, "I want to win $25,000 on *Worst Cooks in America*™" As mentioned in another chapter, I'd already been a contestant on that show the year before. While I enjoyed getting to know the cast, crew, producers and the unique experience overall, the actual filming had been more like "hell's kitchen" than a comedy cooking show for me. Therefore, I had consciously neither thought about nor talked about it anymore. But subconsciously, I must have concluded that since I had been given a second chance to live again, perhaps I could get a second chance at making it a "Heaven's Kitchen" experience, including winning $25,000! LOL!!

The inspirational and glorious music and the joyful God Support joined with fun and fantastic family support. The more beauty there was in interactions with kind doctors, nurses, aides and even the cleaning crew in the midst of positive, rejuvenating and beautiful surroundings, the more I was blessed to be a blessing, even during what seemed as if it should have been the worst of the worst conditions. What made all the difference was in being blessed to be a blessing. I could not help but say as many "God bless yous" as my struggling whisper voice could speak…or sing.

TBBBAB: To be blessed, be a blessing.

TBIYTC: The best is yet to come.

Chapter 8

CHOOSING JOY
AND LAUGHTER

*He will yet fill your mouth with laughter and
Your lips with shouts of joy"* (Job 8:21).

How can you choose joy when you're in the worst of the worst of the worst situations? This impossibility is only possible when you are filled with the Holy Spirit.

*"But the Holy Spirit produces this kind of fruit in our lives: love, joy, peace, patience,
kindness, goodness, faithfulness, gentleness, and self-control.
There is no law against these things!"* (Galatians 5:22-23).

Choosing joy is easy when life is good, but only when God lives in your heart can you choose joy when life is not so good. To choose joy is not to be in denial when you're in a joy-less situation, but to be in faith with assurance that your life is in God's hands; you know, without a doubt, no matter what happens, God is in control.

We can try our best, work, work, work, believe, believe, believe, but some things happen that are beyond our control and threaten our joy no matter how much we work and believe.

However, we always can choose how to respond. The natural response to the joy-less things in this world and in our personal lives, is to get angry, frustrated, anxious and maybe even give up and give in to misery. The supernatural response is to choose joy and laughter with a heart filled with faith. Evil cannot control what is in our hearts when we embrace the joy of the Lord to give us strength, peace, endurance, power and victory over all that seeks to harm us.

When we choose joy, we are recognizing that our burdens are far too great for us to deal with in our finite human understanding, but deep within our hearts we know that nothing is too difficult for God. To choose joy is to surrender our burdens to the Lord to handle, and to submit to His help when we cannot help ourselves. Our enemy loves when we try to deal with joy-stealers by ourselves and hates when we cast all our burdens on the Lord.

"Let him have all your worries and cares, for he is always thinking about you and watching everything that concerns you. Be careful—watch out for attacks from Satan, your great enemy. He prowls around like a hungry, roaring lion, looking for some victim to tear apart. Stand firm when he attacks. Trust the Lord; and remember that other Christians all around the world are going through these sufferings too" (I Peter 5:7-9).

Sometimes things are good, sometimes they are not. Whether good or bad, we can choose joy because our joy is not dependent on the things of this world, but on our trust in the Lord in and through all things. Yet in the ICU how could I have chosen joy when I was not really conscious or capable of choosing anything?

Whatever is in the heart will manifest in some way, whether we are conscious or unconscious. God helps those who cannot help themselves. So even when we are not consciously aware, His joy in our hearts sustains us. When we are unable to consciously choose joy, God also works through "joy-givers." In the ICU, it was primarily through my joy-filled daughters who would choose joy for me when I was too weak to choose all by myself.

You have nothing to lose when you choose joy, but everything to gain. Choosing joy helps heal your body, mind and spirit. To choose joy is to choose life. It is a choice with miraculous power. One profound reality when choosing the joy of the Lord is that the intensity of our pain can magnify our capacity for joy. How can that be? Because it is not when life is easy that we are closest to God, it is when life is most difficult. The presence and power of the joy of the Lord is greatest when we need Him the most.

"The Lord is close to the brokenhearted and saves those who are crushed in spirit"
(Psalm 34:18).

Since the Lord is the source of our joy, the closer we are to Him, the better we know Him, and the deeper we know Him, the greater our joy will be. The deeper our pain, the greater our need of Him; the greater our need of Him, the closer He is to us, and the greater our capacity for the most joy. That is why some of the most joyful people you'll ever meet will be those who have been through the most "stuff."

If wealth, comfort, and a pain-free existence make people joyful, then why aren't there more joyful celebrities, tycoons, and healthy people who have everything their hearts desire? I became aware of this phenomenon when I was in college and was sent as a representative to Harvard and New York where wealthy kids gathered to pretend to solve world problems through a model United Nations activity. I had never been around so many joyless young men and women. They had been raised with "everything" but seemed to have "nothing."

Our joy is not because of the battles, but because of the victory we know is ours.

> *"Many are the afflictions of the righteous, But the LORD DELIVERS him out of them all* (Psalm 34:19; NASB 1995; emphasis added)

> *"I have told you all this so that you will have peace of heart and mind. Here on earth you will have many trials and sorrows; but cheer up, for I have overcome the world"* (John 16:33).

To choose joy is an ability God gives to each person. It is a choice of your heart. First you must choose Jesus to be your Lord and Savior by inviting Him into your heart. Then you must choose to trust in Him with all your heart. Then you must believe His Word is true and take His promises to heart. Your heart determines the course of your life.

> *"Guard your heart above all else, for it determines the course of your life"* (Proverbs 4:23).

A joyful heart is especially important when we are physically ill. What strengthens and heals us spiritually also heals us physically. A joyful heart is a heart God can and does heal. (More on that later in this book.)

My daughters made the choice of joy for me by creating a joyfully beautiful oasis of family photos, music, joyful stories of love and happiness, flowers, cards and balloons. I chose joy in my recovery by focusing not on my troubling condition, but instead upon the joy of those I love. I chose joy in the visions of beauty from the window wall overlooking a majestic river with magical dolphins and magnificently beautiful skies creating cloud formations that looked like angels watching over me, and sunsets that were like explosions of joy reminding me of God's beauty: *"The heavens declare the glory of God; the skies proclaim the work of his hands"* (Psalm 19:1 NIV). All that declares His glory fills my heart with great joy, healing joy!

I chose joy through inspirational music, when not worrying about anything; when praying about everything; when giving thanks through everything, and when thinking on good things:

> *"Don't worry about anything; instead, pray about everything; tell God your needs, and don't forget to thank him for his answers. If you do this, you will experience God's peace, which is far more wonderful than the human mind can understand. His peace will keep your thoughts and your hearts quiet and at rest as you trust in Christ Jesus...Fix your thoughts on what is true and good and right. Think about things that are pure and lovely, and dwell on the fine, good things in others. Think about all you can praise God for and be glad about"* (Philippians 4:6-8).

I even chose joy when a nurse made a mistake that resulted in my blood soaking me, my bed, and my very favorite, wonderful down-filled pillow Rachel had just brought to give me joy. I could choose joy because Rachel was there at just the right time to discover it and immediately run for help from a different nurse who fixed the problem and saved my life – again.

There was so much joy in my ICU room that all the stuff I was going through just didn't seem worth dwelling on. I had a heart of joy even as I lay immobile on an uncomfortable bed. I was unable to eat or drink after the tube was removed from my throat; needles were painfully sticking in my neck, arms and ankle, and one arm had swollen twice it's normal size. I was given a grim prognosis that I would almost certainly suffer from prolonged cerebral, physical, and neurological damage after serious oxygen deprivation. I would have to pass a swallow test before I could eat or drink again. In a room filled with pain and impossibilities, I chose joy and was perpetually filled with the strength of the joy of the Lord.

The more you go through life-threatening, painful, and overwhelmingly challenging things in life, the more you learn the meaning of the phrase: "Don't sweat the small stuff!" If we let the little things in life, what's unimportant, and the simple annoyances disrupt our joy, it not only prevents a joyful heart, but also it drains us of needed emotional and the physical strength to victoriously defeat the big concerns of life on earth. Comedian George Carlin said it best: "Don't sweat the petty things, and don't pet the sweaty things."

When you choose joy, it is only natural for there to also be lots of laughter.

Laughter in the ICU? Oh yes, indeed! Laughter has been widely recognized as the best medicine.

Laughter not only helps the heart, but an ordinary heart that chooses joy becomes an extraordinarily merry heart. A merry heart helps the good doctors, nurses, medicine, and machines work even better.

Laughter is a gift from God. Heaven-inspired laughter is not ridicule or sarcasm, it's knowing that "stuff" happens, so move on. Laughing about crazy things that you cannot control just makes everything better. Our choices in challenging situations can be: 1) laugh and be glad, or 2) get mad and feel bad. One option helps your heart heal better; the other makes it worse. If you want to feel better when you are really feeling bad, if you want to heal better when you are really sick, choose joy! We can laugh even when things are so ridiculously awful that we know nobody but God will make a way when there seems to be no way, and we have lived long enough to see it happen time and time again.

After the most difficult day in the hospital, it was laughter that saved the day. My birthday was to be my discharge day and things just were not going the way they should. Rachel and Melody came late in the afternoon with a birthday gift that helped me survive what I had endured. It was a personalized birthday greeting from my favorite comedian, Trey Kennedy, and I was able to laugh my way out of my pain.

It is so very good when hospitals create healing spaces where patients can get a break from pain and enjoy laughter. I am reminded of the doctor known for laughter, "Patch Adams" (Dr. Hunter Doherty (1945 -) who encouraged laughter among staff and patients which helped suppress suffering and inspired an atmosphere of joyful healing.

Benefits of laughter include:

1. Relieves stress.

2. Stimulates your heart.

3. Enhances intake of oxygen.

4. Increases endorphins in your brain.

5. Stimulates circulation.

6. Aids in muscle relaxation.

7. Improves your immune system.

8. Just makes you feel good.

There is nothing bad; there is only good with laughter.

Did you know that God laughs?

Since we're made in God's image, we are created to laugh. Laughter is the natural response to the joy of the Lord in our hearts.

"But you, God, break out laughing;" (Psalm 59:8 MSG).

"But the one who rules in heaven laughs." (Psalm 2:4 NLT).

"But the Lord just laughs..." (Psalm 37:13).

It was not just the obviously joyful blessings in the ICU that caused me to laugh, it was also in the unexpected and bizarre. Some things caused us to laugh, not because they were so "good" but because they were so "bad."

It was funny for me to try to talk after the tube was removed from my esophagus. Whisper speaking was not easy, but I wanted to do so constantly, as if to prove I could still talk. The humorous content of my "whispered ramblings" when I was under the influence of powerful drugs resulted in a lot of laughing in the ICU.

One such instance was when I became aware of far too many needles in my neck, arms and ankles and tried to take them out. Fortunately, Rachel was standing beside me and prevented my successful removal of those bothersome intrusions, but my response was to sternly admonish her in a motherly tone as if she were a child. In my strongest and firmest whispering, I declared, "Honey, I do not *want* them there!" Not only did my reaction cause Rachel and Melody to burst out laughing, but still causes us to laugh just recalling this incident.

Another funny moment occurred when Daniel saw me for the first time in the ICU. Daniel lovingly stood by my bed while holding a beautiful bouquet of flowers that he said he'd handpicked to ensure I'd enjoy the best.

As Daniel sincerely and somberly spoke encouraging words while handing the flowers to me, my eyes were fixed on them with an intense gaze. I reached for them with my swollen arm while Daniel spoke words of hope and healing.

I was determined to hold the bouquet, but the movement of raising up to do so caused me to cough, which led to vomiting a grotesque gray matter. Rather than be repulsed by the gruesome sight, they all laughed while Melody reached for a suction gadget to alleviate and clean it up. Even yucky stuff can make us laugh. And I would laugh, too, when later seeing the video of this unusual flower saga.

It was funny how much I wanted to whisper-sing and what songs I chose. The topics of my conversations were also funny, like the cooking show story I mentioned earlier. I turned into a senior version of what had been my favorite doll that was popular when I was a kid in the 1960s, Chatty Cathy™, which would talk when you pulled a string behind her neck. It was as if something was pulling my string so I would talk all the time and exercise my vocal chords to fully heal.

A lifetime of laughter had prepared me for a such a time as this. Sixteen years before our family was laughing together in the ICU, we had hearts of joy over Daniel's success in overcoming meth addiction when in recovery in California after the intervention. Because of his deliverance from drugs, we were so happy and joyful; he looked and felt so good and had a hopeful future. We took Brad, one of his friends, out to dinner and were laughing so much that Brad said he'd never been with a group of adults having so much fun without drinking alcohol. It gave a refreshing meaning to what the Bible says:

"Don't be drunk with wine, because that will ruin your life. Instead, be filled with the Holy Spirit" (Ephesians 5:18).

Joy Blessing's translation: "Since God created joy, fun and laughter, when filled with the Holy Spirit we can have more fun and laughter than anyone or anything in this world can offer"

"He will yet fill your mouth with laughter and your lips with shouts of joy" (Job 8:2).

"You have put joy in my heart" (Psalm 4:7).

Chapter 9

SURPRISED!

"O Lord my God, many and many a time you have done great miracles for us, and we are ever in your thoughts. Who else can do such glorious things? No one else can be compared with you. There isn't time to tell of all your wonderful deeds" (Psalm 40:5).

"Everyone was gripped with great wonder and awe, and they praised God, exclaiming, 'We have seen amazing things today!'" (Luke 5:26).

"**Y**our eyes are BLUE!" exclaimed Rachel, looking at me from the chair where'd she'd been working on business for her KYDS Children's boutique. She grabbed her phone to take a photo of my normally hazel eyes that were now blue. Melody joined her in amazement, asking, "How could your eyes change color?" This was to be only one of many astonishing and amazing revelations as the journey of joyful healing unfolded.

It was as if I was having a perpetual surprise party.

My immediate reaction was that the color of my eyes reflected what I had seen when my soul was wandering somewhere out of the earthly realm. I believe that my physical eyes had changed colors because my soul had experienced a dimension I had never witnessed before. I can't shake the feeling that I saw Heaven. I have always thought that just like blue is the color surrounding the earth, Heaven is filled with an unlimited spectrum of shades of blue. I feel that when I was out of my body, what I saw with only spirit vision mysteriously affected the color of my eyes when I returned to my body on earth and reflected the color of Heaven. Of course, I cannot prove this and do not know for certain that the color blue is the substance of Heaven. It's just a feeling in my heart.

For weeks after I had emerged from unconsciousness, the physical world looked different. *Could it be because the composition of my eyes was adjusting to being back on earth?* I wondered. For a relatively brief moment in time, it was as if I was able to gaze into other dimensions of life. Colors were more intense, all living things were of a deeper consistency, and even sounds were sometimes deeply electrifying with piercing vibrations that I felt more with my spirit than with my normal physical senses.

Eventually, my eyes transitioned back to the hazel color which had been mine since birth. The supernatural impressions I'd enjoyed of an extra dimension of earthly existence slowly diminished, and all of what I'd previously known and seen on earth was to look the same as it had before I died.

During my months of recovery, I have been thirsty for more knowledge about how we see things in this world. How might our physical eyes actually change color? I read that change in an environment could change one's eye color. I wondered, *could that also happen with a vision of a celestial environment?* It's possible. I also learned that we only see 1/6th of the color spectrum through our physical eyes. There are other dimensions that we do not see. Science has determined this and developed ways (like night vision goggles) for us to see unexplainable phenomena and what is not visible with the naked human eye. The reality of UFOs is often documented through specially equipped cameras which capture another spectrum of reality, making the invisible realm clearly visible. The more I research this mysterious phenomenon of multi-dimensional life around us, the more I am convinced that my eyes changing to blue reflected a world I witnessed but was not allowed to have conscious memory to recall. The intense color blue from my eyes was certainly a most surprising and mysterious reality when I first became alive again after the miracle.

Having blue eyes was just one of many surprises of shock and awe the first day I was alive again. Most people who would see me that day were as surprised as I was just to see me functioning in the land of the living.

Some would gasp in disbelief; others' eyes would open wide with delight, as if they were watching fireworks or a phenomenal view for the first time, or reacting as if they were seeing a loved one who had been gone a very long time.

One sweet young woman entering my room put her hand over her mouth and exclaimed, "Oh my goodness, oh my goodness, you look so good!" She shared that she'd been watching me for days and thought I was beautiful but never considered such a remarkable recovery would be possible. Her comment was actually reassuring, as I had begun to wonder if perhaps the image of my giant left arm and a preponderance of needles sticking in me in so many places were causing people who saw me to gasp at my frightening appearance.

It was reassuring that the surprising reactions were due to the shock of seeing me so alert and so very much alive. It seems that no one had expected me to ever fully live again.

I had been considered an "impossible" patient, not because my behavior was unbearable or I was difficult to be around, but because it was widely assumed that the likelihood of my walking, talking and enjoying life were slim to none. The most beautiful gasps came when Melody and Rachel walked in to see me sitting up in a chair. They were joyfully surprised to see me functioning normally, as if I'd been through a routine medical event.

I was not yet aware my daughters had been there every day. I was especially happy they had not just popped in to say hello, but they were prepared to stay as long as I needed them. They carried in their computers to set up their office in my room, prepared to be my emotional support and hospital advocate monitoring my care. Their encouraging and supportive presence would be the best therapy and complement to hospital care, and in some ways, literally lifesaving. I was so very thankful for their vital presence. Ever since I was an ever present support for my parents and husband through major medical concerns, I had become keenly aware of the profound healing benefit of companionship in hospitals. Oh, how thankful I was that my daughters were with me through those critical days.

I was also relieved to learn from them that Karly was enjoying the days away from me with good, dog-loving friends who took her on adventures and allowed her to sleep with their children as she did with me. I was so very happy to know that she was well cared for, but I still longed for her to also be by my side. Just the thought of seeing her again was a strong motivation to do whatever I needed to do to take care of myself so that I could once again take care of her.

Health and healing thrive in an environment of love. The love given me from those I deeply loved was the perfect complement to the loving care of the nurses, aides and doctors. I was blessed with an ICU oasis of joyful healing and hope. I not only learned how important this was during the years when my parents and husband endured long hospitalizations, but I also regularly witnessed it when I served as chaplain visiting critically ill patients. Remarkable improvement was always evident when people in the worst of conditions were lovingly cared for by family, friends, and genuinely compassionate doctors, nurses and aides. I was now experiencing first-hand what I had often witnessed to be true.

Rachel surprised me with the most comfortable pillow from her home that for a short while made me feel as if my head lay on a "healing marshmallow of joy." It was sure disappointing when it had to be discarded after being soaked in my blood, as I described earlier.

I didn't just witness looks of surprise at my being alive on the faces of the "parade" of strangers entering my room; there also were the surprises of amazing and humorous things happening to me there.

I was surprised to only be able to whisper and learning it was because I had been breathing with a tube down my throat. I was surprised to learn I had been on life support; surprised to be so thirsty, but not allowed to drink anything; surprised at having had double pneumonia, and surprised to learn I would need what was called a swallow test to ensure I could safely get food and drink to my stomach. I was surprised to have passed the swallow test so quickly, and when told I could then eat or drink whatever I wanted, surprised the nurses when I said I wanted green tea. This made them laugh. I could ask for anything, and all I asked for was green tea. I was surprised to learn how much green tea is particularly beneficial for heart patients and surprised to somehow know it was what my body needed.

It was surprising for me to learn that intubation is such a serious procedure that only 31% of those in my age group of 65-74 survive to hospital discharge after it. Surprise after surprise to actually be alive was realized hour by hour.

The more I learned about where I was and what had happened, the more surprised I was to be alive.

I was greatly surprised to learn that less than 1% of those who suffer sudden cardiac arrest outside of a medical facility survive. Only about 10% of all who have sudden cardiac arrest survive. My very good friend, Claire, who was an EMT and ambulance driver for years, had kept count of the number of people who had survived cardiac arrest during her workdays. She stopped counting when she reached 100 and learned that only two had survived, and that they were the only two who called 911 when they were first having chest pains and did not go into SCA until after the paramedics had arrived.

As my awareness of what had happened and why I was there became a part of my conscious thought, I was constantly surprised to be alive. I was surprised that anyone cared so much to keep me alive; surprised at the extra loving care of the hospital staff; most surprised at how determined my daughters were to ensure the best for me; surprised to be in a room filled with such joy and hope; surprised to see such magnificent views that made me feel as if I were in a luxurious resort, and especially surprised at the river dolphins. I was surprised to not be hungry after learning it had been at least five days since I had last eaten pizza with Carson.

I was surprised at Kevin's look of disbelief when he came in my room with Gavin and Carson, whom I was so very pleasantly surprised and happy to see. Carson and Gavin were the only ones I saw that first day of consciousness who did not look surprised themselves when they first saw me. *After all, didn't they pray for me to live and not die?* They demonstrated the most profound faith in in my recovery to not just survive, but to thrive.

When I called Daniel, he reacted in a surprising way that reminded me of when he was a child and surprised over the abundant joys of our latest adventures. I was surprised to learn he and Gabi had visited me just a few days before and to know how bad I had been when he had visited, which explained why he was so surprised to see me when I made a Facetime™ call to him. It was surprising to be able to enjoy the most wonderful and happy conversation with him while I lay there alone in the ICU. I was surprised to realize after that uplifting and inspirational interaction with him and Gabi and Theo, that it had only been two weeks earlier that I had enjoyed the most fun day at SeaWorld™ alone with Theo. We petted and fed stingrays, laughed together at funny sharks, walruses, and sea lions, and had fun playing with dancing dolphins, and riding the Slimy-Slider six times. How grateful I was that God allowed me that wonderful day with him without having had a heart attack! It was a surprising revelation that God in His great mercy did not let that happen when I was alone with Theodore or any of my grandsons. My prayer is that those surprisingly wonderful times together with my grandsons will continue to happen many times again.

When I saw photos and videos of Daniel praying for me while I was unconscious, I was surprised how my mind immediately thought of the time

16 years before when I was praying for him when he was unconscious from a drug overdose. It reminded me of how when we cannot pray for ourselves, God will impress upon others to pray for us. My prayers led to the restoration of my son's life may years ago, and now God was using him to help me once again fully live.

I was surprised to get mail and gifts that made me feel truly alive and surprised to know I had not been forgotten by those I loved and had not seen for many years. I kind of felt as if I was enjoying the flowers and special recollections of others that are normally a part of memorial services after someone has died. I was happy to have not stayed dead so I could enjoy flowers and fond memories with loved ones and still have opportunities to make more eternally significant memories.

I was surprised by a visit of a hospital chaplain who was a kindred soul. For 11 years after my husband died, I served as a corporate chaplain which included visiting employees in their workplace and in the hospitals. My first hospital visit as a chaplain was after a call that an employee's young daughter was in a coma, as I said earlier. To see a child suffer is the deepest of heartaches. I did not feel qualified to comfort and help this precious little girl and her family at such a time. I most definitely was not, but the Holy Spirit within me responded to my surrendering to His Will. Words of comfort flowed from my lips with ease and love. I had not met this particular family since I had only been a chaplain a few days, but since I had been through the deaths of my parents and husband, and myself been through a major life threatening surgery when I was just 7 years old, my heart was familiar with the intensity of emotions and concerns in such situations when words are never adequate to help, but prayers and the comforting presence of others are desperately needed. I felt compelled to lay my hand on her head and shoulder and pray for her to be healed and fully recover. As mentioned in that earlier chapter, I didn't stop for a moment to consider whether I should pray for total healing, I just did it.

"Such a prayer offered in faith will heal the sick, and the Lord will make you well"
(James 5:15).

Nothing happened; she didn't awaken from the coma. I was becoming rather discouraged that sometimes when we pray, we do not realize expected answers. *But why would God not allow this child to live?* I wondered. *Is it OK to ask God why?* So I prayed again for this little girl and started the drive home. When home, I was startled out of my grief by an unknown caller. I answered to hear the joyful voice of this little girl's mom tell me her daughter had awakened just after I left. It was now more than 20 years later, and I was surprised to be thinking of this little girl responding to my prayer to live, just as so many had prayed for me to live.

Rachel said the chaplain who had visited me in the ICU reminded her of me.

I whispered for the chaplain to sing a song. She joyfully did. I could barely speak in a whisper, but was able to clearly sing along with my chaplain sister:

There's not a Friend Like the Lowly Jesus©

> There's not a friend like the lowly Jesus. No not one. No not one.
> No one else could heal all our diseases.
> No, not one. No not one.
> Jesus knows all about our struggles,
> He will guide 'til the day is done.
> There's not an hour that He is not near us.
> No not one. No not one.
> No night so dark, but His love can cheer us.
> No, not one.
> (Johnson Oatman, Jr., (1856-1926) and George C. Hugg (1848-1907))

I was surprised that even though talking caused me to cough and have chest pain, I *wanted* to talk. I surprised Claire with a call to tell her I was in the hospital and was surprised to learn she already knew. I thought of her when staring at the glorious skies and views from my window, as we regularly enjoyed therapeutic lunches at picturesque locations for our friendship therapy sessions. We called them CJ/JC lunches- the first two initials for our first names, the second two for Jesus Christ. JC always was present at our therapy sessions. I was surprised to see cloud formations that looked like angels while talking with her on the phone, just as we would often see during our heavenly lunches when we conversed about everything and enjoyed venting all our concerns to each other without fear of condemnation since we share the same convictions. CJ/JC lunches were always encouraging and supporting for each of us. I was surprised it was the same when merely talking with her on the phone from my hospital bed.

Claire is a kindred soul whom I met when her son and his fiancée asked me to be their wedding officiant. It was rather uncanny that the day I died just happened to be the 6th anniversary of her son's wedding. Claire was babysitting for them as they celebrated. It was surprising to be able to enjoy such a joyful and wonderful healing friend therapy session with her while in the ICU.

It was surprising to talk with my sister, Susan. Just a year earlier she had survived a heart attack after she lay bloody and bruised on her bedroom floor for six hours before being discovered by her daughter, Pam. I was surprised by how much my heart was blessed by them and surprised to realize that just as God had not let my sister die, He also had done the same for me. What was most surprising was to feel the "breath of Heaven" in an atmosphere filled with God's love. To experience love is to truly live, for that is why God created this world:

"...God .... richly provides us with all things for our enjoyment" (I Timothy 6:27).

But the things in this world cannot be enjoyed without trusting in God, not in things. For the things in this world without God are just things. Our enjoyment is made possible only through what God can give us, and God's greatest gift is love.

Love brings life to the things in this world. I could have been recovering in the most beautiful, colorful, flower-filled room, on silken sheets covering a mattress with divine comfort, and with my head on the softest down-filled pillow, looking at a large screen high definition television inside and glorious views of mountains, rivers and oceans outside. It would not be enough without love.

For things on earth to be enjoyed, they must be shared in an atmosphere of Heaven. The "breath of Heaven" I felt in the ICU was not because all I was going through was perfect and enjoyable. The joyful, healing spirit in my room was because of the love of family, friends, doctors, nurses, aides and others who lovingly cared for me, helping me see that all things infused with the love of God could be enjoyed no matter where you are or what is going on.

Even when I sat alone in the ICU, connected to all sorts of mechanical gadgets to keep me alive, I found joy in what was not an enjoyable situation. It was a place where I realized the love of God in a way I could not, had I been comfortable and in need of nothing. I was to experience the Living Word of God to give me hope, to realize that He actually did love me.

"The Lord is close to the brokenhearted; he rescues those whose spirits are crushed" (Psalm 34:18).

"......For God has said: 'I will never fail you. I will never abandon you.' So we can say with confidence, The Lord is my helper, so I will have no fear. What can mere people do to me?" (Hebrews 13:5-6).

"God has shown His love to us by sending His only Son into the world. God did this so we might have life through Christ. This is love! It is not that we loved God but that He loved us.... Dear friends, if God loved us that much, then we should love each other. No person has ever seen God at any time. If we love each other, God lives in us. His love is made perfect in us. "He has given us His Spirit. This is how we live by His help and He lives in us" (I John 4:9-15 NLV).

In the ICU I was surprised to be alive, but most of all, I was surprised by LOVE.

And I am convinced that nothing can ever separate us from God's love. Neither death nor life, neither angels nor demons, neither our fears for today nor our worries about tomorrow—not even the powers of hell can separate us from God's love. No power in the sky above or in the earth below—indeed, nothing in all creation will ever be able to separate us from the love of God that is revealed in Christ Jesus our Lord" (Romans 8:38-39).

Chapter 10

MERRY HEART MOMENTS – MHMs

"A merry heart does good like medicine" (Proverbs 17:22 KJV).

"Thirty percent"

"What does *that* mean?"

"Your ejection fraction is 30 %"

"Ejection what...?" It sounded like Greek to me.

The kind and compassionate cardiac physician's assistant went on to patiently explain what this meant: "Your ejection fraction tells how well your left ventricle is pumping. A low EF indicates the heart muscle is having trouble pumping blood. You had what is called a 'widow-maker.' This means your main artery was 100% blocked. The lack of blood supply to your heart caused permanent damage affecting blood flow."

I had already been a widow more than 20 years, so it seemed rather humorous that a widow could also have experienced a widow-maker. Why do they still call it that? Just the term "widow" is frightening because of the association with a deadly spider! Death is serious, but when recovering from death, I wanted to focus on life. So as my PA discussed what could result in my death, I prayed for what to do to keep living.

I was happy that Rachel had accompanied me to the test which would measure exactly how much my heart had died, and how much of it was still beating. No one had been with me for a prior swallow test to determine if it was safe for me to eat and drink. Unfortunately, I had been forgotten, sitting in a wheelchair, in a basement hallway for more than an hour after that test was complete. Therefore, Rachel made certain that I would not be alone for any other out of my room adventure. The image of my struggling, yet still beating heart moved her to tears. She took a video of the imaging screen and later showed it to me. It made me weep to see the miracle of my once-dead heart fighting for renewed life with every beat.

The Bible tells us in the King James and New International versions that we are "fearfully and wonderfully made." The New Living Translation interpretation explains best how I was moved to praise the Lord when seeing my beating heart: *"You made all the delicate, inner parts of my body and knit me together in my mother's womb. Thank you for making me so wonderfully complex! Your workmanship is marvelous—how well I know it"* (Psalm 139:13-14 NLT).

The results of the imaging test indicated a *grim* diagnosis. It was *not* surprising to learn of the condition of my heart. It was surprising that I was learning about it while still on earth.

"Your heart experienced the worst of heart attacks. Therefore, most of your heart tissue died."

"Dead? How am I able to talk to you now?"

For a few moments I was silently attempting to understand how I could live if most of my heart was dead.

"So what exactly does 30% ejection fraction mean?

An EF lower than 40% is considered heart failure; 30% is considered severe heart failure.

How does it feel to hear news like this? Well, for me I didn't feel anything. I was numb. I felt as if what I was hearing was not real.

"What now God?" was my silent prayer. I asked the PA, "So, can the dead part of my heart grow back?"

"It's possible that some heart cells can regenerate, but highly unlikely."

"OK?"

I did not want to be alone when hearing the results of the test. I was thankful the PA who was assigned to tell me such troubling news was at least compassionate, patient and sincerely interested in my life.

The Holy Spirit is known as "The Comforter" and there's never been a time I needed comforting more than those moments of realizing I had genuine heart failure. I did hear a comforting, still, small voice of the Holy Spirit speak to my heart that it was going to be alright. That's the same voice and message that Gavin heard when he did not know I had already died. I was at peace because I knew that alright means ALL right.

"You are at extremely high risk of having another heart attack, so you will need to be fitted with a life vest before you can be discharged," the PA said.

"Life vest?"

I thought life vests were what you wear on a boat. Was I on a *sinking ship?*

"The life vest is to be worn 24 hours a day. It is designed to detect if you have a heart attack and will respond with defibrillation." A portable defibrillator! WOW! I was going to be a "bionic woman!" Wearing an electronic vest was a daunting reality which I was not enthusiastically anticipating.

"So, how *long* do I have to wear this? A week?"

"A minimum of three months. Your EF will be checked again in August, and if it is not improved, you will need an implanted pacemaker."

Something inside of me said *there has got to be a better way!*

"Thank you, God bless you," I said softly as the PA left my room.

Laying in my uncomfortable hospital bed, I gazed out at the sliver of a blue sky that I could see if I turned my head just the right way. Since, I had graduated from the ICU room with the inspirational view to one with no view, I no longer had an opportunity for a joyful boost of seeing the "heavens declaring the glory of God," which had been heart healing during my first week at the Heart Hospital.

Trying to find something beautiful to gaze upon outside the window from my new room was as difficult as trying to find a way for my heart cells to rejuvenate, but neither was impossible. I found a way to see a little beauty and light from that not-so-beautiful viewless dark room. I would find a way to experience beauty and light in my not-so-beautiful-and dark prognosis. Just as angels were to light my journey through the dark valley of death, Jesus would light the way during my joyful journey forward.

For as long as I can remember, I have never given up on trying to find a way when there seemed to be no way. When it comes to disease, I believe that God has put something in this world to help us to defeat whatever the enemy uses to try to kill and destroy us. This minor issue of heart failure was no exception. God can always make a way when there seems to be no way.

"Is anything too hard for God?" (Genesis 18:14)

So, I asked for "God's prescription" for my heart to heal. Again, a still, small voice spoke to me:

"A merry heart does good like medicine" (Proverbs 17:22 KJV).

I had memorized this verse in Sunday School more than 60 years ago. Now this verse was God's response for me to embrace as my heart saving life "prescription."

The Hebrew word for "merry" is *meah,* which means joyful, merry or glad. This exact word is also used one other time in Proverbs 14:13: *"A happy face means a glad heart; a sad face means a breaking heart."* I was moving forward to make my heart glad, believing that my most effective heart healing medicine would be JOY!

Joy is to the heart what the heart is to joy. They are better together and essential for life. My heart needed to be full of joy to thrive, and joy was absolutely necessary for my heart to survive.

I was prescribed essential pharmaceuticals to keep my heart beating. But "joy" was my prescription to keep me living. God did not bring me back into this world merely to survive a little longer with a "dead" heart. The same power that raised me from the dead is the same power that could – and would – restore my heart with renewed determination and purpose to shine as a light of hope in this dark and hopeless world.

If God's Word referred to joy as medicine, then joy was to be my primary medicine to restore my heart. Everyone has a choice to believe the Bible is the Word of God or not, but the only choice for me is to believe that when God says something in the Holy Scriptures, that settles it.

Each day, I prescribed for myself doses of "joy pills" in the form of MHMs-Merry Heart Moments. MHMs were the primary prescription for my newly created personalized cardiac rehab: "MHM Therapy." Unlike all my other medicinal prescriptions, MHMs had only one side effect: laughter.

When my children were little, I taught them to sing the words to Proverbs 17:22 and had composed a tune for them to do so, which I have also taught to my grandsons. This song has become the theme song for MHMs therapy:

> "A merry heart, does good like medicine,
> like medicine is a merry heart!"

The foundation for successful MHMs therapy was to consistently and constantly think on good things as much as possible:

"Fix your thoughts on what is true and good and right. Think about things that are pure and lovely, and dwell on the fine, good things in others. Think about all you can praise God for and be glad about" (Philippians 4:8).

The good things I experienced, witnessed, and heard about were to be what I would take to heart.

> *"For as he thinks in his heart, so is he"* (Proverbs 23:7 NLV).

> *"A heart at peace gives life to the body"* (Proverbs 14:30).

To cultivate a merry heart is not to be in denial of all the problems in the world or in my life. To cultivate a merry heart is to be in faith in God's power of healing, victory, and purpose in and through it all. It is to believe what God says in His Living Word about the heart and joy.

So, I surrendered my fears of being electrocuted when wearing a life vest and dismissed all thoughts of needing a pacemaker or of living the remainder of my days on earth with heart failure. I took some prescribed medicines and worked to maintain a positive attitude when dealing with the side effects, such as blackouts, weakness, muscular aching, ringing in the ears, nausea, rashes, blurred vision, dizziness and fainting. However, my MHMs therapy included weaning myself off of medications that were essential during and after cardiac arrest, but were not to be "forever pills" for me.

Part of my MHMs therapy involved study and online research of articles and gleaning insight and wisdom from YouTube™ channels hosting dozens of cardiologists and other medical and nutritional specialists relating heart healing supplementation, diet and lifestyle.

I also searched for online testimonies from cardiac arrest survivors, but after discovering how few survive, and how those who do make it to hospital discharge were only those that received immediate help from medical professionals, there wasn't any "merry" in that information. I also tried to find info on anyone who had been revived with two defibs, but that was even less "merry." In the few studies I did locate, about three of 10 were successfully revived, but 10 of 10 did not survive until hospital discharge. As I was finishing this book, I did find favorable conclusions from a four-year study with paramedics in Canada that was published in late 2022. While it was good to read at least some promising use of two defibs, there wasn't enough "merry" in my research about heart failure patients for it to be a part of my MHMs therapy.

The Bible was my "joy as medicine" textbook and guide. My primary, primary care physician (PPCP) was Dr. Jesus in his role as Dr. Jehovah Rapha. The well-known meaning of Jehovah Rapha is "God who heals." The heart of the meaning of that Hebrew word is: "to mend, repair, or restore something to its normal or useful state". In other words, "to fix what is broken". Dr. Jehovah Rapha and Dr. Jesus would fix my broken heart, and I never had to wait for an appointment. They were available for consultations 24 hours every day, 7 days a week, including holidays. There is a benefit to have doctors who never sleep and never need a vacation.

Part of MHMs therapy was to realize I had to avoid heartbreaking concerns. It's not that I wasn't to care about others, but to recognize that my damaged heart could not take on too much heartache, at least for a while. During the years when I devoted myself to the care of my parents, children, husband and served as a chaplain, I was often so burdened for the concerns of others that I would get chest pains. I learned how important it was to first cast all my personal cares – as well as the cares of others – upon the Lord to handle. If burdens can harm a healthy heart, then the cares we do not immediately give God to handle will cause even more serious damage to a sick heart. The best way for those with or without heart issues to demonstrate the greatest care is to faithfully pray for the cares of our family, friends, others and ourselves while still being used of God to help whenever we have the means to do so. Jesus said to cast *all* – not just *some* – of our cares on Him. God does not help those who help themselves, but those who trust in God to help them. We are never to think that we are capable in our own limited power to handle the cares of this world. As a heart patient, I found that it was heart healing to demonstrate the greatest care for others when devoted to praying for anyone and everyone, and actively engaging in MHMs and conversations as much as possible. There are times when we must share heartbreaking concerns with those we love, but we can do so without breaking our hearts.

Another MHMs therapy element was to modify listening to bad news of any kind. There has always been and always will be bad news in this fallen world. Just as a person without heart failure must be careful in how much of each day is consumed with "doomsday" news, a person with heart failure cannot risk a mental diet of too much bad, bad news. Although we must all be aware of what's going on in the world that affects our lives and how best to deal with major concerns, we cannot be consumed with them. We must seek to focus on ways God has for us not to be overcome with evil, but to overcome evil with good. MHMs therapy seeks to always learn of more good news of victories over bad news.

Since my MHMs therapy began while I was still confined to a hospital room, I was determined to make the most of it. First was to use the time between shots and tests to meditate on the Word of God and everything we are promised for health, healing protection, peace, joy, love, deliverance, provision and help in the Bible. Concurrently with this was to talk to Dr. Jesus and Dr. Jehovah Rapha a lot. Every time I consulted with my physically present doctors I would also be in conversations with my ever present spiritual PPCPs about every medical procedure. My PPCPs would help me understand what my other physicians told me, and give me answers to questions about my heart such as: What does this mean to me now? How do I live like you want me to when I am often so weak and in such great need?

MHMs therapy involves a history of remembering and thanking God for merry heart healing memories of the past. It involves current events by cherishing and thanking God for the merry heart healing blessings of the present, and MHMs therapy involves prophecy, by anticipating healing merry heart moments God has promised for the future.

"For I know the plans I have for you, says the Lord. They are plans for good and not for evil, to give you a future and a hope" (Jeremiah 29:11).

I also knew there would be times I did not feel like thinking on good things or choosing joy in circumstances that were overwhelmingly not joyous. That was OK; at times when I was weak or discouraged, God would chose joy for me in the unexpected ways as He has promised:

Each time he said, 'My grace is all you need. My power works best in weakness.' So now I am glad to boast about my weaknesses, so that the power of Christ can work through me. That's why I take pleasure in my weaknesses, and in the insults,

hardships, persecutions, and troubles that I suffer for Christ. For when I am weak, then I am strong heart (II Corinthians 12: 9-10, NLT).

Even without heart failure, anyone can sometimes become too weak to deal with overwhelming life concerns, but when trusting in the Lord during and through hardships, we realize His strength is perfect when our strength is gone. The joy of the Lord becomes our strength through our weakest moments. God's strength causes us to truly have a merry heart and motivates us to focus on MHMs. Paul encouraged believers suffering in Corinth to understand this wonderful truth:

"Since I know it is all for Christ's good, I am quite happy about "the thorn," and about insults and hardships, persecutions and difficulties; for when I am weak, then I am strong—the less I have, the more I depend on him" (II Corinthians 12:10).

There is much more that God has taught me about MHMs therapy than I have room to write about in this book, but it's important to share the most helpful and fun part of my MHMs therapy which involved/involves participation from anyone willing to share MHMs with me, beginning while I was hospitalized.

I refer to MHMs as "joy pills," so I would ask those who came into my room to share with me an MHM to help heal my heart. Everyone was happy to do so, including doctors, PAs, nurses, aides, janitors, etc. Those blessing me with heart healing MHMs were also greatly blessed with a heart of joy themselves.

Some of the "joy pills" that helped heal my heart included: A nurse who did a "Riverdance" in my room several times because it is what she most loved to do; an aide who shared the MHM of when she was adopted from an African orphanage at just nine years old and became a part of a big and wonderful family in Jacksonville, and a young nurse who greatly blessed my heart one difficult night when I could not sleep. She shared the MHM of her love of singing and how it was her dream to sing on Broadway. When I asked her to sing in my room as if living that dream, she began singing Carson's favorite song, *Awesome God*©. She would regularly continue to help heal my heart with inspirational MHMs singing throughout the nights whenever she had a break.

Whenever Gavin and Carson came to see me, just their presence in my room gave me perpetual heart healing MHMs. They shared MHM jokes and funny things they had done. They made me MHM cards with colorful hearts and MHM words. Gavin told me the MHM of his first place win at a tennis tournament, then shared some MHM laughter as he pretended to have forgotten to bring his winning medal to show me, but pulled it out of his pocket. Melody brought me the most delightful MHM when she walked in with my much loved grand-doggy, Archie! Even Archie gave me the most heart healing "joy pill" MHM when he would lay on my chest over my heart as if he knew it was greatly needed. His MHM kisses and MHM wagging tail were, indeed, heart healing. Archie only weighs five pounds so he could easily be brought into my hospital room. I wanted MHM Karly there, too. While Karly was too big to bring into the hospital, Melody shared the MHMs of photos of her looking happy and having fun with dog loving friends.

Rachel brought me food MHMs. Happy food makes the heart happy. She and Melody brought me salmon and salads with ginger and other delectable heart healthy treats. Just the presentation of food can be a most delightful MHM. Rachel understood this when she brought me a MHM offering of a beautiful ceramic bowl full of plain Greek yogurt topped with organic blueberries shaped into a smiley face, with a golden spoon to eat it. Delicious MHM food was not only a culinary treat, but also fed my heart with MHM nutrition. My heart craved MHM food. Since the heart attack, I had a heightened awareness of what was MHM food and what was not.

Melody brought me a MHM canvas painting that I had made in 2020 of Psalm 91. Just after she placed it on the windowsill, a nurse's aide came in and pointed to it as I asked her if she would like to share an MHM. She smiled while reading the words of Psalm 91. She shared with Melody and Gavin and me the MHM of how those words had saved her life when she was trapped in a collapsed apartment building during the Mexico City earthquake many years ago. She was not even a Christian at that time and did not know the words she was seeing were in the Bible, or how they "happened" to appear. Reading those words over and over during the hours before she was rescued, encouraged her; she was rescued physically and saved spiritually.

A most amazing MHM was when Melody brought me my "read-through-a year" Bible from my condo. This is a Bible that lists a passage from the Old and New Testaments and one psalm to read every day so that you can read through the Bible in a year. I was interested to know what the designated scripture passages had been for April 23rd – the day I died. When I saw what it was, I had MHM tears and MHM laughter. The passage for April 23rd was Psalm 91! I wept while my eyes were drawn to the promises in Psalm 91 that I experienced on that fateful day:

> *"Those who live in the shelter of the Most High*
> *will find rest in the shadow of the Almighty.*
> *This I declare about the Lord:*
> *He alone is my refuge, my place of safety;*
> *he is my God, and I trust him.*
> *For he will rescue you from every trap*
> *and protect you from deadly disease.*
> *He will cover you with his feathers.*
> *He will shelter you with his wings.*
> *His faithful promises are your armor and protection.*
> *Do not be afraid of the terrors of the night,*
> *nor the arrow that flies in the day.*
> *Do not dread the disease that stalks in darkness,*
> *nor the disaster that strikes at midday.*
> *Though a thousand fall at your side,*
> *though ten thousand are dying around you,*
> *these evils will not touch you"* (Psalm 91:1-7, NLT).

And MHM visions of the angels who were with me in death flashed in my mind as I read:

> *"If you make the Lord your refuge,*
> *if you make the Most High your shelter,*
> *no evil will conquer you;*
> *no plague will come near your home.*
> *For he will order his angels*
> *to protect you wherever you go"* (Psalm 91:9-11, NLT).

One morning, I was battle weary and wanted to be out of the hospital. That day I was just too tired to focus on MHMs, for I was weak from enduring too many discouraging and disappointing realities, too much coughing, too much chest pain, and too much focusing on what might be instead of all that God was doing. As I lay still, feeling kind of like I was in the twilight zone and most in need of a little boost from Heaven to reignite MHM therapy, a beautiful young woman walked into my room and said what I had heard many say during my hospital stay.

"Do you remember me?"

I just smiled as she shone as a light from Heaven at me. I didn't remember her but sensed a joyous connection. She was "Dr. Find-A-Way," who was used of God to bring me back to finish the good work God had begun in my life. God sent her to me as an MHM booster "joy pill."

What a joy it was to talk with her, to learn how she was not supposed to have been at Beaches Hospital that day but had been called to go there while headed to another hospital. It was then I also learned she was a believer in Jesus as her Lord and Savior and had prayed for me during and after the miracle that had changed her life as it had mine. Her mother told her that God must have something special planned for my life. I reminded her how it was obvious that God's hand was on her life; God had ordained a most wonderful medical ministry for her. I assured her that God was smiling upon her and thanked her for how willing she was to allow God to use her to save my life. I was about to pray with her when the privacy curtains began to move and out emerged a singing MHM little boy with a stethoscope around his neck and carrying a pint-sized doctor bag.

"Dr. Theo is here," said the sweet voice of my three-year-old grandson, Theodorable. I introduced him to my emergency room doctor. Moments later, I had the joy of introducing her to Daniel, Gabi, and Gabi's smiling mom from Brazil. MHM smiles and photos followed as the MHMs overshadowed the despair I'd been fighting since the middle of the night before.

Dr. Theo made me laugh constantly. I didn't care if my chest hurt and I coughed more when I laughed. Any pain seemed so insignificant when compared with the bountiful MHM laughter.

"Let me check your heart. Yes, Jesus is in your heart," was confidently diagnosed by Dr. Theo. He then checked my bones and gave me a "shot" with a syringe from his doctor bag. "You're gonna be OK, G-Joy! God is healing you," Dr. Theo joyfully declared.

I could feel my heart healing.

Theo then brought me a hat for my birthday present and clapped his hands while singing *Happy Birthday* to me. My birthday wasn't until days later, but it seemed as if his words were reminding me of my new "birthday" of April 23, 2022. My first birth was in 1955 when I entered this world. My second birth was when I was "born again" into the family of God in 1960. Daniel and Gabi followed Dr. Theo's singing with an MHM song they spontaneously made up together while Theo danced.

Shortly after they'd left, I had an MHM visit from a hospital PA named Amy. She revealed how she was with me the first day I was transported to Baptist Heart Hospital. She also was part of a women's prayer group who had responded to Melody's call for prayer. She gave me MHM joy pills when sharing how she had monitored my progress even after she was off duty the week I'd been in the ICU. She had prayed for me every day and assured me that I had the most wonderful God inspired care. Even the woman assigned to clean my teeth would sing along with the hymns, worship and praise songs from my phone.

More and more my heart was filled with MHMs that were a part of a miracle. The long, lonely and difficult hours of my hospital journey were filled with beauty and joy through perpetual MHMs. I felt my heart healing when hearing of MHMs of growing relationships; about how one woman had been told for 12 years that she would never have children and then had twins who had just celebrated their fourth birthday; another joyfully shared the MHM of moving to Jacksonville, meeting the love of her life, getting a home and starting a family, and a PA enthusiastically shared how much she was looking forward to the first vacation to Disneyworld with her young children.

There's just something "heart-healing" about hearing the MHMs of others. Joy-filled stories of life are heart healing.

Cherished MHMs were also shared with me on social media from those I had not seen for years. One of my favorites was from pilot Tim, with whom I had always enjoyed working when I was a flight attendant. Tim surprised me with an MHM of how I had blessed him in ways I never realized. Other MHMs were from nieces I had loved and care for when they were little and who had not forgotten me; from others I had worked with in my multiple jobs, and MHMs from brides and grooms I had married, recalling their beautiful wedding ceremonies and joys of marrying the loves of their lives.

After the hospital, every day shared with my grandsons was a huge dose of MHM "joy pills." Every CJ/JC lunch with Claire was a MHM feast filled with laughter and love. The more I looked for MHMs, the more MHMs looked for me, and the more I could feel my heart healing.

A merry heart blesses another with merry healing. MHM therapy is not just good for those with heart failure, but is essential for sustained health and healing within everyone. While I needed extensive MHMs to heal my heart, just ordinary doses can help prevent heart failure for anyone.

One extra special and wonderful MHM was generously offered by my favorite and most exceptional nurse, April. She knew how much I wanted and needed a break from the stale hospital environment. She understood how much I missed the views that had been heart healing in the ICU, and how much my heart needed fresh air, needed to gaze at the river dolphins and sky, and to get a breath of life that was not possible in my hospital room. So, she joyfully volunteered to make it happen after she finished her 12-hour shift. Just thinking of going outside was an MHM. Just seeing her bring a wheelchair to pick me up was an exhilarating MHM. My daughters going with me outside was a double MHM. It was a glorious MHM to sit on the veranda overlooking the sparkling river and artistry of the sky that had been so heart healing for me in the ICU. Not only were the MHM view and delicious outdoor air rejuvenating my body, soul and spirit, but so too were the wonderful, joyful MHM conversations with nurse April and my daughters. It was truly an MHM gift from Heaven.

It was especially heart healing to realize how April had already given me exceptional MHM care through her regular nursing duties, but still joyfully desired to give more. MHM nurse April had still more MHMs to share with me the next day. My hair had become a tangled mess during my nearly two weeks there, so when Rachel said she was bringing some dry shampoo to clean my hair, nurse April volunteered to braid my hair. Again, after serving patients throughout her 12-hour shift, she came to my room in the evening and helped my heart healing by styling the most beautiful MHM braid I had ever had. With each MHM, it was as if God's finger would touch my "dead" heart with healing joy.

On my 67th birthday, I was scheduled to be discharged. That was a birthday gift from God. Having read that very few who initially survive what I experienced then make it to hospital discharge, it was especially a day worthy of a significant celebration, but it started with circumstances making it difficult to focus on any MHMs. Despite my hopes, a joyful MHM celebration outside the hospital was not to be, but my day was blessed with an MHM flower arrangement shaped like Karly that my sister Susan and niece Pam sent. I felt as if Karly was somehow with me. But the best MHMs showed up when Gavin and Carson brought me delightful gifts, such as chocolate covered strawberries and orchids. The MHM birthday explosion of joy was magnified when Melody walked in with a precious and adorable MHM birthday doggy, and there was lots of MHM laughter in watching a personal birthday greeting Rachel gave me from my favorite comedian, Trey Kennedy.

I will reveal later just how a year of MHM therapy resulted another amazing miracle, but after just one month, the positive healing benefits of MHM therapy were already evident.

The electrode pads under the life vest had caused an irritating rash on my back and I was having other problems which brought me back to the hospital. While undergoing evaluation, tests and treatment, there was some wonderful news. My EF had only been 30% on my birthday, but after just one month of MHM therapy, it was between 35-40%. This meant that I would no longer need the life vest or a pacemaker. So, it was obvious to me that my MHM therapy had been the right choice for me. It was also another confirmation that God's Word is true. Medicine is good, but joy makes it better.

Joy is to healing what healing is to joy!

Chapter 11

HEART MUSIC

"He has given me a new song to sing, a hymn of praise to our God. Many will see what he has done and be amazed. They will put their trust in the LORD"
(Psalm 40:3, NLT).

"Remember what Christ taught, and let his words enrich your lives and make you wise; teach them to each other and sing them out in psalms and hymns and spiritual songs, singing to the Lord with thankful hearts" (Colossians 3:16).

Music is to the heart as the heart is to music. What this means is that just as a healthy heart requires a rhythmic beat to sustain life, it is the contents of our hearts that create and choose the rhythm of music that affects every element of our lives. "Heart music" inspires the sounds of life that can help heal and bless our hearts. In Biblical Hebrew, the heart refers to where we make choices motivated by our desires. Therefore, if we love the Lord with all our heart, it is filled with the joy, love, and peace that inspire the music of life to positively impact the healthy functioning of our hearts.

We celebrate our birthdays with a song; every milestone and activity of life is filled with music. God created music for our enjoyment as well as to inspire, comfort and bless us. Just as a life without a heart is no life at all, so is a heart without music.

When my daughters ensured that my favorite inspirational songs, hymns and spiritual songs were playing constantly in the ICU, they understood that just as music filled my heart with joy before I died, the joy of music would help heal and restore my heart when I was alive again. Music is a pure and delicious honey to my soul and a blessing to every cell of my physical body. Sound is powerful. Even when sound cannot be heard, it is in the air doing far more than we realize.

There have been numerous studies proving that music is good for plants, so why not people? One such observation that conclusively proves the power of sound vibrations through music was at the Barcelona Opera House during Covid lockdowns, when the musicians filled the concert hall with plants since people were unable to attend their concerts. The instrumentalists played their glorious music with only plants "listening." All were amazed at how the plants grew bigger and stronger after weeks of "soaking in" the vibrations of magnificent orchestrations.

Sound waves of voices, instruments, devices and nature bless us in ways that are, in a sense, miraculous. As I've been writing this book, I've experienced the sounds of a fountain outside my window, the birds singing, visions and sounds of ocean waves on my videos, all of which inspire me in ways that are real but I cannot explain.

Growing beside the main speaker that fills my condo every day with the sounds of my favorite music, there is a fir tree that was only about two feet tall when first placed there. In just two years, it has grown to almost six feet. An identical tree purchased at the same time and planted in a back yard of my daughter's house is still only about two or three feet tall.

Many medical professionals recognize the blessings of music. One of my favorites is wise and wonderful brain surgeon, Dr. Ben Carson. He became famous as the first to successfully separate conjoined twins. He also listens to classical music while operating.

The positive benefits of sound is a topic for another book. For this book, I know that God, who created the invisible emotions of love and joy to bless us with health and healing, most certainly created sound waves to be instrumental in doing so as well. My personal "scientific" experience is in knowing how the music my daughters ensured would be playing day and night in my hospital room permeated the cells of my body to help heal in ways that cannot be expertly explained, except to conclude "why not?"

It was not only the reality of invisible waves of sound piercing the molecular composition of each damaged and dead chamber of my heart to encourage healing, but so too were the vocal declarations of the promises of God singing along with glorious and beautifully harmonious instrumentation.

Words are powerful and words set to music are even more so. The right words with the right music make us laugh, dance, cry, celebrate, rejoice and reminisce.

Some music is genuinely birthed in Heaven, such as Handel's *Hallelujah Chorus*. Handel became deaf at age 41, yet he was able to "hear" in his spirit the power of words and music. When completing *The Messiah*, he reportedly said, "I did think I saw all Heaven before me, and the great God Himself seated on His throne, with His company of Angels." Whenever I am in a performance of the *Hallelujah Chorus*, I stand and weep. There is such power in instrumental music with singing that is not limited just to enjoyment and fun, but also to health and healing.

In Revelation chapter 5, we read lyrics to some of the music in Heaven: *"I heard the voices of thousands and millions of angels around the throne and of the living beings and the elders. And they sang in a mighty chorus: 'Worthy is the Lamb who was slaughtered—to receive power and riches and wisdom and strength and honor and glory and blessing.' And then I heard every creature in heaven and on earth and under the earth and in the sea. They sang: 'Blessing and honor and glory and power belong to the one sitting on the throne and to the Lamb forever and ever.' And the four living beings said, 'Amen!' And the twenty-four elders fell down and worshiped the Lamb"* (Revelation 5:1-13, NLT).

Those who have died, seen Heaven, and come back to talk about, tell of the perpetual glorious music and singing in our celestial home. If music is woven through the atmosphere of Heaven, then it must be very important for blessing life on earth.

Just as music is the inspiration for our eternal soul in Heaven, it has the same power to rejuvenate one's physical body and emotional spirit on earth. In Heaven there is also perpetual and unceasing perfect health. So, is it any wonder that music and health are also interconnected on earth? Just as the heart is the foundation for our physical lives, the heart of music blesses our soul and spirit, and also the physical composition of our hearts. Studies have shown that not only do plants thrive in environments of inspirational music, but so do people and animals. We cannot see or feel music, but we are blessed in the effects of it. The invisible power of music blesses our heart, soul, mind and body. Music is one of the most profoundly obvious ways we realize how much what we do not see is responsible for what we do see. Without music, life is just "noise." The way a heart has rhythm and gives us life reminds us of the way the rhythm of music gives us abundant life. If Dr. Ben Carson considers music to benefit his brain functioning to perform miraculous surgical procedures, then music is powerful beyond what we can yet know or explain.

How else can we explain the reaction of crowds to music at sporting events, concerts, business and political events, and in church – if not for the impact of music upon the heart?

The benefits of invisible sound waves make an impact whether or not they can be heard with our natural senses. These vibrations not only impact people, animals and plants, but are also known to pierce the atomic elements of all matter. Certain frequencies can break glass and cause movement of inanimate objects. I consider it reasonable that while I was plugged into machines in the ICU, even they functioned better in that atmosphere permeated with sounds of love and joy. It makes me consider the possibility that every Word of God is to be of the most glorious sounds.

Some theologians believe that God started the world with a song. Creation could very well have occurred through the music of heavenly orchestration set to the voice of God. So in my humble opinion, the physical world can still be renewed, restored, and even infused with life through music.

I believe I'm living proof of the profound and yet mysterious interconnection of music and healing.

It's particularly interesting to note how Christianity is the one religion in the world that is associated with magnificent, glorious and harmonious music. Many religions are known for chants and monotonous moans or worshiping and conjuring powers from their counterfeit gods through beating on drums in a trance-like state. I believe Christianity unleashes ultimate blessings of our most High God above all gods through the most phenomenally powerful and beautiful music that generates joy, strength, hope, healing and love in the hearts of believers. As music has strengthened my heart time and again, I cannot sing of the greatness, faithfulness and love of God without smiling.

While I listen mostly to praise and worship songs and hymns, my MHMs therapy also includes beautiful, uplifting, fun and inspirational music from a variety of genres, including classical masterpieces and songs by smooth and melodious voices such as Michael Bublé, Elvis, and country crooners.

Music and singing are mentioned throughout the Bible, such as when the Israelites sang and danced after escaping the Egyptians when God parted the waters of the Red Sea; David playing his harp to chase away the evil spirits from King Saul; Mary's song after being told by an angel she would give birth to the Messiah; Paul singing for joy in prison, and the book of Psalms which were written to accompany music. Music energizes, comforts, inspires, celebrates, encourages and blesses us with the ability to glorify God with our voices and instruments. Music is essential for living with a heart of joy.

The world tries to create a counterfeit alternative to health and healing and joy. One such way is through getting drunk with alcohol. Alcohol in excess can give temporary artificial joy of mocking laughter and obnoxious singing. While alcohol may seem to help heal emotional and relational issues, it results in headaches, hangovers and diseased livers and hearts. The Bible tells us there is an alternative to what the world offers us to attempt to heal our hearts, mind, body and emotions, and it involves music and singing:

> *"Don't be drunk with wine, because that will ruin your life. Instead, be filled with the Holy Spirit, singing psalms and hymns and spiritual songs among yourselves, and making music to the Lord in your hearts"* (Ephesians 5:18-19, NLT).

Music is in your heart, and unlike the fake and temporary substitute for joy of alcohol, there can be sustained health and healing when you are being filled with Holy Spirit inspired music.

The Bible tells us that God gives each of us our own "heart music:"

> *He put a new song in my mouth,*
> *a hymn of praise to our God.*
> *Many will see and fear the Lord*
> *And put their trust in him"* (Psalm 40:3, NIV)

Our hearts sing with thankfulness:

> *"Remember what Christ taught, and let his words enrich your lives and make you wise; teach them to each other and sing them out in psalms and hymns and spiritual songs, singing to the Lord with thankful heart"* (Colossians 3:16).

The day before Jesus was crucified, He sang:

> *"And when they had sung a hymn, they went out to the Mount of Olives"* (Matthew 26:30).

God sings:

",,,He will rejoice over you with joyful songs" (Zephaniah 3:17, NLT).

I agree with many theologians who teach that God started the world with a song. Decades ago, I was drawn to listen to and sing along with a musical composition which expressed the convictions of my heart entitled: *God Gave The Song©*.

> You ask me why my heart keeps singing;
> why I can sing when things go wrong,
> but since I found the source of music,
> I just can't help it; God gave the song.
>
> Come walk with me through fields and forests;
> we'll climb the hills and still hear that song;
> For even hills resound with music;
> They just can't help it; God gave the song.
>
> What's that I hear? I still hear the music;
> Day after day, that song goes on;
> For once you know the source of music, you'll always hear it....
> God gave the song.
> Come on and join – it's the song of Jesus;
> Day after day, that song goes on;
> For once you know the source of music; you'll always hear it......
> God gave the song;
> For since I found the source of music, I can't help singing,
> God gave the song.
> (Gloria Gaither, Ronn Huff, William J Gaither, 2013, Capitol CMG Publishing)

The birth of Jesus Christ on the earth resulted in musical celebrations throughout angelic realms *and* every dimension of our physical world.

The most popular song at Christmas, *Joy To The World* – reminds us that as Jesus fills our hearts, we sing:

> Joy to the world, the Lord is come,
> let earth receive her King,
> let every heart prepare Him room
> and Heaven and nature sing…

The atmospheres of both Heaven and earth are permeated with miraculous sounds that infuse life, love, joy and peace into all creation, so that the universe is filled with *heart music*.

As we live on earth, we can join in singing with the choirs of Heaven and of nature. If we are to believe in God's Word, not only does God sing, but angels sing, humans sing, and plants, trees, flowers, mountains, rivers, oceans, stars, sun, moon and animals somehow "sing" for joy with us! All creation is filled with heart music that energizes and motivates us to truly live with a heart of joy.

Chapter 12

ALIVE! BUT AM I REALLY LIVING?

"The thief does not come except to steal, and to kill, and to destroy. I have come that they may have life, and that they may have it more abundantly" (John 10:10, NKJV).

"...for through him God created everything in the heavenly realms and on earth.
He made the things we can see and the things we can't see—such as thrones, kingdoms, rulers, and authorities in the unseen world. Everything was created through him and for him" (Colossians 1:16).

Just as my eyes had changed color from hazel to blue after I'd died and come back to life, the way I was seeing things had also changed in the first few months following my heart miracle.

Colors seemed to be in a deeper dimension than I'd seen before. Flowers seemed as if they were about to sing. The shapes of trees assumed a unique architectural design to resemble images from *The Hobbit©*. When I would gaze in some directions, it was as if I saw what is normally invisible!

Simple spoken words were of richer tones of musical blends of melody and harmony. The diverse elements of food became more evident as I developed a heightened sensitivity to what was good for my body and what was not.

At times, I felt like I was in another world.

When I was awake, I was having visions of seeing beauty originating in a different realm. When I slept, my dreams were of landscapes and vistas and homes of phenomenal beauty in an atmosphere of indescribable delight. Had I seen Heaven? I knew I was alive, but was I really living? Was I actually still alive in this world which had been my dwelling place for 67 years?

Or was I just imagining still being here?

There were some moments during my initial weeks out of the hospital when I wondered if I was just dreaming about everything. Was I in a coma with delusional thoughts that I was involved in living through normal life? Or was I lying in a dark isolated room on life support, trapped in a dimension between life and death?

It wasn't just the beauty of life that was magnified; my awareness of the disappointments was also enhanced. My chest pains became more intense when I was alone in my condo and missing Karly. Since I did not yet have strength to carry Karly up and down the stairs to take her outside several times a day, the girls felt it best that others would continue to care for her. So along with enhanced beauty, there was also an awareness of deep pain within my dwelling place, now devoid of my constant companion who'd been there before I died. Even though my disappointment and longing for Karly were deep, the anticipation of her returning motivated me to do whatever I needed to do not just to survive, but to thrive.

The first night back at the place where I lived with Karly, I felt very much alone. I knew God was with me, but sometimes we need God to show up through animals and people who make us feel more alive. Since I was perpetually questioning whether or not I was actually living during those first days outside of the hospital, I was feeling uncertain whether or not all that was around me was true reality.

On that first day out of the hospital, I was so exhausted I slept for 14 hours straight without awakening even once. It wasn't just my physical body that was battered and bruised, but I was emotionally spent, spiritually weak, and mentally depleted. It's not easy to die and come back to life with a body, soul and spirit in need of total rejuvenation. Sometimes there just weren't enough MHMs to keep me energized to do all I wanted to do. What I needed most was MHM rest and physical renewal

The first morning awakening in the condo, I fully expected Karly to be there with me. For a moment, I started to get up to take her out for a walk. Shocked into reality, I knew I was still too weak to care for Karly alone.

It was my heart's desire to be out of the hospital in time to join my family on Mother's Day, which was only two days after I settled into my personal rehab environment. I was ready to go several hours before Rachel was to pick me up. During those hours alone waiting for my ride to Mom's Day brunch, my cardiac "Joy therapy" was primarily to rest in the Lord while watching many hours every day of Bible teaching online, including: David Jeremiah, Jack Hibbs, Daniel Moritz, Kevin Zadai, Jentzen Franklin and many other messages about prayer and Heaven and near death experiences. I also enjoyed having a "window to the world" through videos of the world's most beautiful, fun and fascinating places and animals that reminded me of how much I wanted to be healed to fully live again.

While exercise was restricted because I easily became dizzy and tired, my body, soul and spirit were growing stronger one day at a time by merely gazing out the window from my condo at the sunrise, the moon, and birds while "havin' a little talk with Jesus," and watching seven sparkling colors of a rainbow form around the fountain within about a hundred feet from the condo.

I didn't like being totally alone in my condo, so I was especially anxious and excited to finally see Karly after having been gone so long from her. I was also enthusiastically anticipating spending joyful time with Gavin, Carson, and Archie. My prayers had been answered to be able to celebrate a few hours on Mother's Day with them.

Gavin and Carson were the first to emerge from the stairs leading up to my condo, carrying flowers and smiling in their adorable Mother's Day light blue suits with palm tree prints. Rachel brought more flowers. Because of my enhanced awareness of dimensions of color and beauty, these bouquets seemed more extraordinary than any I had ever received before. Flowers represent the beauty of life, so the more flowers around me, the more alive I felt.

Rachel was driving what I call her "cupcake car" because it is such an unusually delightful color that it reminds me of how I feel when looking at a decorated cupcake. Cupcakes are just fun to look at and consume. Rachel's car was fun to look at and ride in.

While she drove over the inter-coastal bridge en route to her ocean side club in Ponte Vedra Beach, I gazed out the window and felt as if I was looking at a rare painting that had come alive.

The waves glistened with enhanced beauty and life. What was different? This was not the same as I remembered. *Am I alive?* I wondered.

The laughter of my grandsons touched my heart with MHMs that I actually felt were restoring life to each cell, little by little, one moment at a time, *but was this a dream-or was I truly alive again in the world I had known before I died?*

Normally, when dining in a restaurant alongside the ocean, all I want to do is look out the windows. That Mother's Day, I couldn't stop staring at each movement of my grandsons. They reminded me of dolphins – smiling all the time. They were excited to give me their handmade cards and gifts. Gavin was excited to give me a ceramic heart and flamingo he made for me after knowing I was alive again and recovering in a hospital. The boys made me laugh when they said, "This is your lucky day," and then presented me with ten lottery tickets. I won ten dollars from those tickets, so no life changing influx of bountiful financial provision. I had already won the biggest lottery of all. My prize of life was far superior to mere monetary gain.

While feasting on food which exploded in my mouth with deliciousness and which I passionately enjoyed as if I had never eaten before, I did glimpse at the sea. Again, I felt as if I had to be in a dream seeing marine life emerge from the gently crashing waves that no one else could see. It kind of reminded me of an animated Disney film in which sea life would assume human-like conversation and characteristics.

These moments of Heaven on earth were heart healing in ways that no medicine could ever be. Although there were moments of continued feelings that I may have been imagining it all while laying comatose elsewhere, I was determined to enjoy every moment of the imaginary life while hoping that it was real.

After dinner, I went to the Crismond home of Rachel, Kevin, Gavin, Carson Karly and Archie.

Karly and Archie were waiting when the door opened. I held Karly for the first time since we had separated. I assured her of my love. As I stroked her fur, my fingers seemed to be floating on curly marshmallows. Karly's and Archie's smiles and happy eyes permeated my consciousness with an explosion of delight. Karly seemed different; we had not been separated for such a long time since I had been in New York City for the filming of a television show. As our hearts reconnected, it was as if those feelings of love were encapsulated in unlimited joy molecules of blessings infused into each cell of my being. Each wet kiss from her scratchy tongue, each movement of her constantly wagging tail was heart healing Heaven sent "ice cream" for my soul. Karly's and Archie's smiles and enthusiasm to see me made me feel so loved. If I was just dreaming, I didn't want to wake up.

I could not yet take Karly back with me to our condo, so the joys of our temporary reunion would have to sustain me until I was able to care for her totally and completely again. Basking in the afterglow of a wonderful Mom's Day celebration, I fell asleep shortly after Rachel dropped me off. I peacefully drifted off to sleep in my "dream world," praying the realities of delight I experienced that day would never end, even if it meant I was imagining it all.

The next day, my supernatural vision began to slowly wane, just as my eyes had transitioned back to their color from birth. The pain, problems, and challenges of our fallen world would gradually overcome my awareness of seeing dimensions of extraordinarily magnificent beauty and indescribably amazing delight.

For just a little while, a brief precious moment in time, I feel as if I could have been allowed to see things as God created them to be before the fall of humanity through the sin of Adam and Eve. I had not been dreaming or in a coma, but I had been able to view some of life on earth through Heaven's eyes. *Could it have been a reflection of what I had already witnessed in Heaven while I was absent from my body? A glimpse of eternity?* Perhaps.

"No eye has seen, no ear has heard, and no mind has imagine what God has prepared for those who love him" (I Corinthians 2:9).

Although evil has corrupted all things in this world, within all creation there is an element of beauty still evident in the way God had originally created everything. Maybe my journey through the portal of death and back had briefly awakened an awareness of the deeper dimensions and multiple realms of God's creation that the god of this world, who has clouded our mortal vision, has made it impossible to see.

I believe that my death allowed me briefly to see past what C.S. Lewis is famous for referring to as "Shadowlands". What is eternally real is blurred. We cannot yet see the reality of what God has awaiting us of unblemished, indescribable beauty and amazing wonder.

"Now we see things imperfectly, like puzzling reflections in a mirror, but then we will see everything with perfect clarity. All that I know now is partial and incomplete,

but then I will know everything completely, just as God

now knows me completely" (I Corinthians 13:12, NLT).

It became evident that God allowed for me to get a glimpse of eternity because the months following my death were not an easy road.

Following that glorious Mom's Day was the beginning of a journey of pain and joy, but one of both doubt and discovery of the blessings of the promises in God's Word.

Day and night, I dealt with both shooting pains emanating from my heart and dull aching chest pain with periodic frightening heart palpitations. The only way I could fall asleep at night was to perpetually listen to music reminding me of God's promises. When pain, discouragement and weariness were too frightening, my prayer was merely, "Help, Lord," while listening to song after song of the healing promises of God: *Heal Me*© by Terry MacAlmon; *Songs of Hope and Healing*© by Don Moen; Prestonwood Choir Radio, Maranatha Singers Radio, Discovery Singers Radio, Hymns4 Worship, Bob Fitts radio on my online apps and stations with hours of calming voices reading healing Bible verses and psalms.

My cardio rehab included starting each day with an uplifting, energizing and hopeful MHM Cardiac Rehab Therapy Playlist:

> *JOY*© -King and Country
> *Today is the Day*© – Lincoln Brewster
> *Tell My Heart To Beat Again*© - Danny Gokey
> *The Battle Belongs to the Lord*© – Phil Wickham
> *The Blessing*© – Terry Jacobee
> *Psalm 91, 46, 90*© – Shane and Shane
> *Never Give Up*©; *Dream On*©; *This Could Be the Day*©- Signature Sound
> *Because He Lives*© – Bill and Gloria Gaither
> *Even If*©; *I Can Only Imagine*© — Mercy Me
> *Praise You In This Storm*©; *Here's My Heart*©– Casting Crowns
> *Made Me Glad-You Are My Strength, My Shield*© –Various Singers
> *Be Strong and Take Courage*© – Don Moen and Choirs
> *I Speak Jesus*©- Charity Gayle
> *Prayer Anthem*© - Carman
> *Change My Heart, Oh God*© – Maranatha Music

Even though I was alone with not even Karly by my side, I felt the living presence of God through all these voices joining me in singing God's promises every day. These songs were and continue to be heart healing. Little by little, one day at a time, I was reminded of the joy of the Lord as our strength to live a full and rich life of purpose and hope. Some of these songs were those Gavin and Carson liked when we used to enjoy regular nighttime dance parties. Now these were a part of healing dance parties for me as I sought ways to an abundant life when there often seemed to be no way.

Although, as I said, I enjoy several other genres of music, such as tunes sung by Michael Bublé, classical instrumentalists, a little bit of country, a little bit of rock and roll and pop, for most of the first year of MHM cardiac rehab therapy, I needed to listen mostly to selections from my playlist. Sometimes I felt that just as King Saul was tormented by demons that would not leave him alone until David played heavenly music for him, I needed Heaven-sent music to expel the demons of sickness, disease, and discouragement from me. The more I learned how few survived, let alone thrived after sudden cardiac arrest, the greater my desire and energies were devoted to ensure I was in that "less than one percent club." I wanted the Holy Spirit to keep working in and through me to not just survive but to thrive, and music is part of living a Holy Spirit filled life.

As mentioned in the previous chapter, heart music was a most essential part of my "Joy cardiac rehab" and MHM therapy. After my "praise and worship cardiac dance party" each morning, I would continue to play praise songs, worship songs, hymns and inspirational melodies softly in the background while I worked on weddings, managed housework, prepared meals, worked on writing this book, emailing, etc., and when searching the web for heart health information and watching YouTube™ videos by cardiologists who spoke of all matters related to heart health. Everyone is fearfully and wonderfully made and I was seeking God's wonderful plan for healing me to be all He created me to be for the rest of my life.

I could drive but was reluctant to do so when wearing a life vest. It was daunting just to think of the vest shocking me back to life when I was home by myself, let alone while driving. Everywhere I drove or visited, I was extra cautious to not get too close to people in crowded areas. I especially had to be cognizant of loud noises which could potentially set off the electrodes strapped to my body and knock me out. I was also reluctant to drive much because my car was breaking down nearly every week, which meant I was regularly stranded somewhere on a hot day waiting for a tow truck. At least wearing a life vest sure did keep me praying without ceasing.

There were times I did not hesitate or fear driving at all when my destination was to share G-Joy time with Gavin, Carson or Theodore. It was the merriest of MHM cardiac rehab therapy. They thought it was kind of funny that for a while when wearing the life vest, I was an "electric grandma." The MHM prescription of sharing life with my grandsons was the most effective MHM of all. They somehow all had a special power; whenever I was with them, I never had chest pain nor palpitations. GCT (Gavin, Carson, Theo) medicine was the best of all since the only side effects were perpetual smiles. The same with Archie and Karly. If I was holding one of them, they had "healing fur"; just to touch them was heart healing.

While I still could not have Karly with me at the condo, I was able to be with Archie when Melody was out of town. That helped to fill the void in my heart because of Karly's absence. Melody's home is only one story so there was no concern about climbing steps. Archie also only weighed five pounds so I could easily carry him around. Being with Archie was better than having a resident cardiologist with me around the clock during those initial weeks of MHM Therapy.

At night, Archie would sleep on my heart. He rested comfortably on my sloping chest since I could only rest in a semi-reclining position. If I laid flat, I would have heart palpitations. One night I had a nightmare that the life vest had shocked me while Archie was on my chest, and he went flying in the air. I awoke relieved Archie was still sleeping safely on me, but I took off the vest for the rest of the night as a precaution against possibly electrocuting Archie.

I had been wearing it for almost a month by then and needed a break from it since I had developed an irritating rash on every area of my skin where there was an electrode pad. I was having an undesirable reaction to the life vest - just as I had when taking most heart medications. So I was to widen my search and understanding for what was the best treatment in my unique condition.

For a while, I sometimes awoke at about 4AM with palpitations. Occasionally, the pain was so intense I felt as if I were having another heart attack. When awakening at that hour, I felt it most important to pray not just for me but for whomever and whatever came to mind. It is that time of the day which many believe is a time of spiritually charged intensity, increased warfare between light and darkness. At about 4AM seems to be when there are many deaths. I did not want to be one of those deaths, so that alone was motivation enough to pray even more. Other times during the night my sleep was disrupted. I would awaken from gurgling chest sounds and shooting pains which I got through by praying over and over, "Praise Jehovah Rapha," and, "Help me Jesus," while I increased the volume of heart healing music.

I missed even more the comforting presence of Karly during those long, difficult days and nights. I knew God was with me, but sometimes we just need His presence to be through a beloved dog. The Hebrew word for dog is *kelev* which means "like the heart." The name given for our beloved furry children in the Bible has to do with the heart. Is it any wonder that our hearts are connected to our dogs? Dogs have a sense of knowing us and feeling what we are feeling in our hearts. It's no wonder that my heart seemed to be calmer when I was with Archie and Karly. They were extra cuddly and comforting when they sensed my heart was hurting more than usual.

During those few weeks, it became evident that it might be longer than a few months before I could adequately take care of Karly. It was the first time in more than 30 years that I didn't have a precious doggy child in my home, and I did not like it. Dogs have always been an important part of my life, and I couldn't image life without at least one doggy child. I didn't talk to anyone other than God about what I was going through, but if Karly had been with me, she would have been happily listening to me. In a way, she was with me because she was constantly in my thoughts as a motivation to successfully work through MHM cardiac rehab. The sooner I got better, the sooner Karly could come home. I especially worked on regaining strength and muscular endurance by climbing up and down my stairs so I would have no problem carrying Karly when she returned home. I did not want to go on any walks without her as it was just too sad to walk alone. I had been walking Happy, Karly and Kiwi the nine years I had lived there, and it was just too heartbreaking walking around the neighborhood without any canine companion. I was so excited to soon be taking her on walks again and having her with me day and night.

But it was not to be.

On May 15, 2022, I held Karly on my lap en route to the airport. I cherished every moment on that 30-minute ride, holding her, petting her, talking with her, telling her how much I loved her. She was going to fly to Idaho where

Kevin's sister, Kara, and brother-in-law, Brian, were going be her foster parents until she was all mine again.

She seemed happy with them. Knowing this was both comforting and reassuring to my heart.

They took wonderful care of her and regularly sent me photos of her enjoying life with their doggy, Max. I was happy for her. I was happy for the joys that Karly brought into Kara and Brian's home. I was not happy without her. A most important part of my life was missing.

On July 12, 2022, while I was driving Gavin and Carson to tennis lessons, Kara texted me. My heart began throbbing with grief after I stopped in front of the tennis courts and read her words: Karly was gone.

At first I thought it couldn't be true. She would come back to life as her momma had. She'd been almost dead when paralyzed two years before, but survived at that time to live as if she were a puppy again. No. NO! Karly was not dead! Kara also loved Karly, so when I called her we cried and mourned together.

I soon realized that the walk with Karly the night before I'd died had been our last walk together in this world. The last time I'd held her on the way to the airport had been the last time I would ever feel her heart beat next to mine.

As I mentioned in an earlier chapter, I am convinced that our beloved pets will be waiting for us in Heaven, but we still hurt on earth when they are gone. Although I have pictures of Happy, Karly and Kiwi on the walls of my condo, and cherished memories of sharing love and life with them, I could not avoid the heartache from their loss. My house was not a home without them.

After about a month out of the hospital, the palpitations and chest pains became very concerning. I knew that I couldn't ignore the chest pain anymore and called Melody about midnight to take me to the hospital. In my self-study of heart issues, I had diagnosed myself as having symptoms of pericarditis, and it was not a condition I could take care of on my own. This time when I called Melody to take me to the hospital, I actually remembered doing so and was fully aware of the journey.

I was uncomfortable, but not feeling an urgency to get there as quickly as possible. I just knew that I could not put off doing so any longer. She drove the same route that she had six weeks prior, pointing out where it was I died and milestones of where she had been when talking with the emergency operator and the hospital and Rachel. We talked of how blessed we'd been that it had happened on a Saturday morning when a normally very busy road had very little traffic. On a weekday, she couldn't have made it to the hospital as fast as I needed to be there that first time.

My self-diagnosis proved to be right. My heart was suffering from inflammation – pericarditis. Also, the shooting pains and chest aching were the results of the severe trauma I incurred when the doctors were bringing me back to life.

There also was very good news from a cardiologist I had not seen before and yet who perfectly fit the description of the cardiologist I had prayed for. Dr. Gilani was brilliant yet was able to explain concerns in a patient and non-condescending manner. He truly cared about the way I felt, cheerfully answered questions and concerns, and even let me video his explanation of what was going on with my heart while he drew pictures so I could more effectively understand. He reminded me of my two all-time favorite TV doctors I faithfully watched every week more than 50 years ago: Robert Young on the show *Marcus Welby, MD*© and Chad Everett (aka Dr. Joe Gannon) on a drama called *Medical Center*©. I used to think that if I ever was in the hospital, I would want one of them to be my doctor.

"Dr Welby-Gannon" (aka Dr. Rupert Gilani) also was the bearer of very good news. After I'd been fitted with the life vest, I was instructed that I would need to wear it for at least three months. Expectations were low that my EF could improve enough to not need a pacemaker. Dr. Galani cheerfully informed me that I no longer needed the life vest; after just one month of MHM cardiac rehab, my EF had amazingly improved to between 35-40%!

PRAISE THE LORD! HALLELUJAH!

This was the most wonderful news. The life vest had been causing me not only to have increased anxiety, but the irritating rash also had become much worse. It was very encouraging to know that MHMs work. Of course, this is from my own independent study, but MHM therapy sure worked for me and most assuredly affirms God's Word that a merry heart is, indeed, good, very, very good. I will explain in the last chapter just how good MHM therapy had worked after one year.

It was also good because now Melody was able to plan a belated birthday trip for me to The Polynesian Disney™ resort for two days, and one day at my favorite theme park, Epcot™. If I had still been required to wear a defibrillator life vest, I could not have enjoyed a glorious mini-vacation with all my children and grandchildren. We went swimming, played games and watched fireworks that I'd been told just a few weeks before I might never be able to enjoy again.

Just over a month after being "doomed to a permanently handicapped future," God revealed His plans were consistent with His promises:

"For I know the plans I have for you, says the Lord. They are plans for good and not for evil, to give you a future and a hope" (Jeremiah 29:11).

For the first time since my heart miracle, I did not wonder if I was in a dream, nor did I doubt I would truly live again. I felt more alive than ever.

Everything and everyone made me laugh on that first trip after the miracle, but there was a moment that shocked me and caused my heart to beat extra hard and fast. I did not know Daniel was joining us at the lodge. He decided to surprise me by sneaking up behind where I was lounging and suddenly jumping in front of my face. The girls were great actors in pretending not to see him approaching behind me. Even though it felt like my heart was going to jump out of my chest and I screamed, I was soon laughing about it with everyone. Rachel took a video and I saw that I had the same "bug-eyed" response when we had been standing so close to a lightning strike on the Easter Sunday 6 days before I died. I was determined not to have a repeat of my heart stopping 6 days after Daniel's surprise.

After swimming for hours, playing ping pong, and just having a grand MHM day, we gathered on the resort beach to watch fireworks and play with the boys in the sand. Carson and I remained to play in the sand after everyone had gone back to their rooms. That first day of MHM fun caused me to be on an emotional "high," but I didn't want it to be over and return to my "Karly-less" condo.

After our day of MHMs, I was so filled with joy and excitement that I was the last to sleep and the first to awake just before sunrise. Melody, Rachel, Gavin and Carson were still in dream-world when I ventured outside the room to ensure I would see the sunrise from the beach overlooking Lake Buena Vista.

I sat alone on the lakeside beach, as most guests had still not awakened. I loved talking to my best friend, Dr. Jesus, there. He and I had a lot to talk about while I listened to my cardiac therapy morning playlist.

While doing so, a delightful and unusual big bird swam up close, within about 6 feet in front of me on the edge of the waters. I think my doctor best friend sent him. Standing within just a few feet from me, he opened his wings as if to fly away, and yet began to dance to the song I was playing over and over: *Be Strong and Take Courage.* © I was the only human there! This "angel bird" was dancing for me. I was laughing out loud as his performance lasted for almost an hour. It was a perfect MHM to start this amazing day.

Before leaving the beach, storm clouds were gathering, and the forecast was a 70% chance of rain. As the angel bird danced, I asked God to send the rain away so we could enjoy this one special family day together at Epcot™ where the grounds are covered with beautiful flowers and outdoor vistas.

God did bless the day not only by sending the rain away, but also by "painting" layers of moisture laden clouds forming majestic rainbows. Glorious colors within angelic cloud formations surrounded the seven perfect colors of multiple rainbows creating a visual interpretation of the words in Psalms:

"The heavens declare the glory of God;
the skies proclaim the work of his hands"
(Psalm 19:1).

I have never been anywhere other than Hawaii where there were so many rainbows. The rainbows, the dancing bird, and perpetual MHMs with my grandsons were the perfect "joy pills," the most gloriously wonderful prescription for heart healing from Dr. Jehovah Rapha.

Rainbows are not only magnificently awe-inspiring and beautiful beyond description, but also are a reminder of the promises of God and how He makes all things beautiful in His time. That day it was His time to ignite hope in my heart for the beautiful plan for me and my family. I was not to live as one who is part of the "walking dead" but to be a woman who is 'a walking miracle" with a heart of joy and hope.

The best of medical care is not enough to live with a heart of joy and hope. Complete health and healing are fulfilled through faith and trust in what we cannot see to heal what we can see. Medicine is good, but the prescriptions in the Bible from Dr. Jehovah Rapha are the best!

The day of rainbows was followed by many beautiful days exploring God's purposes and beautiful opportunities for me and my family. My joys were magnified to take Gavin and Carson to tennis lessons each week at the Ponte Vedra Inn and Club. I always have countless MHMs from watching them be and become the best God created them to be on the tennis courts.

I also enjoyed MHM lunches shared together between lessons where we befriended the most delightful server who was a Holy Spirit filled Christian and wonderful role model for the boys. His name was Michael, so he reminded us of Angel Michael in the Bible. We had great conversations with him and learned how he was studying to be an engineer while working full time as a server. We loved hearing about how he met his wife and that she was a surf enthusiast and Christian radio personality. Michael and his wife invited the boys to a Christian surf camp where we had the most glorious MHM morning at Jacksonville Beach where Gavin and Carson surfed for the first time.

The MHM weather was perfect. The skies were painted with the glory of God and the ocean waves flowed as if ordered by the Lord while patient and kind surf coaches demonstrated the servant nature of Jesus to enthusiastic kids. I watched in awe and wonder as God was revealing His love, joy, and beauty to my grandsons and reminding me of His wondrous purpose for my life. I thought of all the joys I would have missed that summer if God had not returned me to this world.

I was happy to be on earth and healthy enough to enjoy a truly momentous occasion in July when we gathered for Daniel's 40th birthday. It was not only a significant milestone in his life, but a pivotal moment in my own for having been a mom for 40 years! The number 40 has much Biblical significance. In the sacred scriptures, 40 symbolizes new life, new growth, transformation, and a change from one great task to another! Could this be more symbolic of my life?

Example of the number 40 in Scriptures include:

- 40 days Noah was on the Ark

- Moses fasted for 40 days before God gave him the 10 Commandments

- The Israelites lived on manna and wandered in the desert 40 years before making it to the promised land

- The Prophet Elijah walked 40 days to reach the mountain of God

- Jesus fasted and was tempted by satan for 40 days before beginning his earthly ministry

- Jesus ascended to Heaven 40 days after His resurrection

The number 40 is also significant in human life as it takes 40 weeks from conception for a boy or girl to be fully ready for birth. Within all the meanings of 40, is the inherent message of being ready for a new life; escape from bondage; freedom to be the best in any situation, and fulfillment of all that God has created us to be.

For God to have allowed me to live to be with my firstborn son on his 40th birthday was a significant indication of how we had survived the "wilderness" and were emerging into new and wonderful opportunities in a "promised land of renewed hope and joy." The rest of our lives was to be the best of our lives. The rainbows we all enjoyed seeing together that summer reminded me of God's faithfulness in and through all things. Even though the enemy had tried to kill each of us numerous times in the previous 40 years, no weapon of death formed against us could defeat the purpose of God. The most magnificent purpose for our lives was ahead and our lives would be as beautiful and glorious as those rainbows if we did not give up and trusted Him with all our hearts, all the time.

Daniel's 40th birthday celebration included dining at Space 2020 at Epcot™, which was significant because 20 plus 20 equals 40. Also, being in "outer space" on Daniel's 40th birthday reminded me of where I had been for almost 40 minutes. We also went to a Tampa MLB game that reminded me of how I was intending to go to Carson's baseball game on the morning of the miracle. We also enjoyed the best steak dinner at a St. Petersburg restaurant that reminded me of how much I enjoyed delicious food more since coming back from death. My favorite part of Daniel's big birthday celebration was when I first saw Theo running towards me with enthusiastic excitement and joy. It reminded me how we should be when coming to Jesus in prayer each day.

The summer joys following my heart miracle were to help me realize that life, indeed, is for living. We are not to allow dreams and passions to die any time before we close our eyes and awaken in our Heavenly home. Heart failure is not meant as failure to truly live a purposeful life with a heart of joy, but to be all God created us to be, one day at a time, until the day we really die.

It would still not be an easy road to be a "dead woman walking." The more value you are to God in your assignment, the greater will be your attacks. I was blessed with a miracle and became a higher level target of the enemy. Therefore, the attacks have been greater after my miracle than those before. I now had a greater assignment for the glory of God in His Kingdom that was disrupting the intent of the god of this world and the kingdom of darkness.

I had been raised from the dead. I was given another chance not just at life, but at living for purposes that matter most for all eternity, not just the miniscule part of my eternal life that is lived on earth. Little by little, every day, Jesus was changing me, and "one day perfect I will be."

Chapter 13

BELIEVE IT OR NOT – GOD RAISES PEOPLE FROM THE DEAD

Gavin and Carson have told me that many of their friends didn't believe their grandma died and came back to life. Perhaps you are also reading this book and are skeptical that it really can or did happen. Believe it or not, God does raise people from the dead. He did in Bible days and still does today.

There is growing popularity and interest in life after death. Such as evidenced by the movie *After Death©*, released in 2023 by Angel Studios about those who have had what is termed a near death experience, or NDE. In recent years, best-selling books have magnified the reality of NDEs, such as *90 Minutes in Heaven©* by Don Piper, and there's the 2014 movie, *Heaven is For Real©*, based on a book written by the dad of a little boy who experienced a NDE. Most people who are dead for a few minutes – or even longer – do not recall memories of anything at all; others like myself recall manifestations of angels. Only about 5% of people who experience a NDE recall what they saw when outside their bodies. That doesn't seem like a significant percentage, but it is significant enough to confirm what the Bible teaches: We are living an eternal life now that will continue after we leave this earth.

In spite of the true-life stories portrayed in movies and books and on popular media channels featuring Kevin Zadai of *Warrior Notes Ministries,* and NDE guests on Sid Roth's *It's Supernatural,* and Randy Kaye ministries, it can still seem to some as unbelievable!

But you don't need to die and come back to life to know that God who gives life most certainly has the power to restore life that He created. Everything that we hear must be validated through God's Word, so since NDEs are in the Bible, and if we believe the Bible is true, then NDEs are to be believed. It really doesn't matter if you believe it or not. God says it, so that settles it.

Many in traditional religious denominations, including those of which I used to be a part, have been taught to believe that supernatural healing and resurrecting people from the dead were only something God did temporarily. Just as there is no mention in the Bible of God saying, "No more," when it comes to praying for healing, there is nothing written in the Scriptures to indicate that the power of God to raise the dead has ever come to an end. If God had a glorious reason for restoring life in Biblical times, He has not changed His purposes for doing so now.

In spite of misguided religious teachings, for as long as I have known about Jesus, I have always believed in miracles and God's resurrection power. God said it, I believe it, that's good enough for me. If God raised people from the dead in the Bible, then of course He can and does do so in our modern times. Why not?

The entire Bible is focused on one man – the Son of God – who would die and come back to life. If our faith is based on a resurrection, how is it so unbelievable that people can be raised from the dead? Jesus rose from the grave three days after He was crucified on a cross for our sins, giving all humanity the choice of eternal life in Heaven instead of eternal damnation in hell. Unlike others who have died and come back to life, Jesus walked and talked on earth with a perfect resurrected body. We, like Jesus, will one day have resurrected bodies, but for those of us who are considered among the "walking dead" on earth now, our souls returned to mortal flesh without awesome superpowers we will someday enjoy in our resurrected bodies.

Since coming back from death, I realized that in the more than 60 years of reading the Bible, I did not give much thought to anyone being raised from the dead other than Jesus Christ. I can remember all my life thinking that the Rapture would happen "any day," so I naturally assumed my life on earth would end when I went to be with Jesus at that time. However, if I died *before* the Rapture, I would go to Heaven and stay there.

Jesus' death and resurrection are evidence of the reality of life after death as the destiny for all who believe in Him.

"Jesus told her, "I am the one who raises the dead and gives them life again. Anyone who believes in me, even though he dies like anyone else, shall live again. He is given eternal life for believing in me and shall never perish" (John 11:25-26).

People of all faiths know the story of Lazarus. He was dead and wrapped in grave clothes, but Jesus merely spoke and raised His friend Lazarus to live again.

"When Jesus arrived at Bethany, he was told that Lazarus had already been in his grave for four days....and many of the people had come to console Martha and Mary in their loss.... Martha said to Jesus, 'Lord, if only you had been here, my brother would not have died. But even now I know that God will give you whatever you ask.' Jesus told her, 'Your brother will rise again.' 'Yes,' Martha said, 'he will rise when everyone else rises, at the last day......' Jesus told her, 'I am the resurrection and the life. Anyone who believes in me will live, even after dying.' Jesus.... arrived at the tomb, a cave with a stone rolled across its entrance. 'Roll the stone aside,' Jesus told them. But Martha, the dead man's sister, protested, 'Lord, he has been dead for four days. The smell will be terrible.' Jesus responded, 'Didn't I tell you that you would see God's glory if you believe?' So they rolled the stone aside. Then Jesus looked up to heaven and said, 'Father, thank you for hearing me. You always hear me, but I said it out loud for the sake of all these people standing here, so that they will believe you sent me.' Then Jesus shouted, 'Lazarus, come out!' And the dead man came out, his hands and feet bound in graveclothes, his face wrapped in a headcloth. Jesus told them, 'Unwrap him and let him go!'" (John 11:1-44).

I encourage you to read all of what is written about Lazarus; it is so much more interesting and inspirational than any counterfeit "walking dead" movie or book.

Other accounts of those raised from the dead in the Bible include:

1. Elijah raised the son of a widow from the dead (I Kings 17:17-22) I feel that when I was widowed, God raised my son from the dead.

2. Elisha raised the son of a Shunammite woman from the dead (2 Kings 4:32-35).

3. A man was raised from the dead when his body touched Elisha's bones (2 Kings 13:20-21).

4. Many saints rose from the dead at the resurrection of Jesus (Matthew 27:50-53).

5. Paul raised Eutycus from the dead (Acts 20:9,10).

127

6. Peter raised Dorcas from the dead (Acts 9:36-41).

7. Jesus raised the son of the widow of Nain from the dead (Luke 7:11-15).

8. Jesus raised the daughter of Jairus from the dead (Luke 8:41,42,49-50).

The most amazing NDE Bible story was given to the apostle Paul. He authored many books of the New Testament about living a life of joy and victory. Religious leaders hated him because he preached that Jesus was the Messiah. Their hatred led to stoning Paul and leaving him to die. What happened when he died sounds similar to many testimonies of those who have experienced an NDE in modern days:

"Let me tell about the visions I've had, and revelations from the Lord. Fourteen years ago I was taken up to heaven for a visit. Don't ask me whether my body was there or just my spirit, for I don't know; only God can answer that. But anyway, there I was in paradise, and heard things so astounding that they are beyond a man's power to describe or put in words (and anyway I am not allowed to tell them to others)" (Romans 12:1-4).

God has allowed many of those experiencing NDEs to talk about the details, but many others, like Paul, have been instructed to *not* tell everything they witnessed. I can understand why. Not only could it tempt us to become proud and arrogant when we return to our flawed physical bodies where we still struggle with a sin nature, but also it would magnify the greatness of the things that occupy our eternal home more than the One who created it. God made certain Paul would not be tempted to be prideful when he returned to earth to fulfill his mission and he wrote:

"That experience is something worth bragging about, but I am not going to do it. I am going to boast only about how weak I am and how great God is to use such weakness for his glory. I have plenty to boast about and would be no fool in doing it, but I don't want anyone to think more highly of me than he should from what he can actually see in my life and my message.

"I will say this: because these experiences I had were so tremendous, God was afraid I might be puffed up by them; so I was given a physical condition which has been a thorn in my flesh, a messenger from Satan to hurt and bother me and prick my pride. Three different times I begged God to make me well again.

"Each time he said, 'No. But I am with you; that is all you need. My power shows up best in weak people'" (2 Corinthians 12:7).

What Paul shares helps us to also understand one of many answers to one of life's most perplexing questions: "Why does God allow us to go through painful stuff?" Well, God uses all things – even pain in this temporary world – for good. Believe it or not, our enemy always wants to destroy our *temporary* blessings to tempt us to lose our joy of investing in *eternal* treasures. However, we can live with a heart of joy no matter what happens, since we are assured that *all* things work together for good for those who love the Lord and are called according to His purposes.

One day, there will be no more pain, but it is through our pain that we can realize a magnified capacity for joy as God's presence is magnified in and through it all. The ones who have the capacity for the greatest joy are those who have known the greatest pain. Even pain can work for the good of those who know, love, and serve the Lord. Pain is not good, but the peace and joy of God in and through pain are good. It is not in comfort and ease that we develop hearts filled with great joy; it is when we are in the most weak and disabling or painful conditions that God's power, joy, and hope are greatest because that is when He – the God of joy and peace – is closest to us. If we don't need God because everything is just fine in our lives, then most often we will not experience all that God can do in and through us.

Even if one is confined in a hospital room, God shows up as the source of joy, strength, peace, and power to a magnitude not possible if we had never known pain. How else can you explain that the most joyful, content, and even happiest people are those who have been through the most "stuff?" When you are in a situation that *only* God can handle, the door of your heart opens to receive the power of God to a magnitude you could not realize if you are always living "your best life now."

It is important to understand that it is not only those who actually see visions of Heaven and/or have a conversation with Jesus that are considered to be blessed, but it also is those who "believe without seeing."

"…Then Jesus told him, "You believe because you have seen me. But blessed are those who haven't seen me and believe anyway" (John 20:28-29).

I also believe that God is allowing us to experience and learn about more miracles in these "last days" before the Rapture so we will not give up when surrounded in hopeless situations in our "last of the last days world." Miracles strengthen our faith by reminding us of the power of God to overcome anything. Miracles also help us to know that what we see with earthly eyes is not *all* there is. So many shockingly bad things we don't understand are going on in the world that it's reasonable to assume God would allow more and more shockingly good things to remind us of His power to overcome and be victorious in and through it all.

Our enemy is flooding our awareness with zombie stories of supernaturally empowered humans and aliens and warfare in "outer space" and drawing our children into a life-consuming interest in the powers of evil through countless magical stories under the guise of entertainment. All of this is a distraction from the genuine power of God that we possess when the Holy Spirit lives in us. Everything that children, teens, and adults are seeing manifested through movies, books, videos of magic and unearthly powers, is satan's counterfeit of the powers of Almighty God to distract us into believing that the power of man and evil is greater than the ultimate power of the God above all gods.

The forces of evil do possess powers that are awe inspiring to those who do not know the Lord. This has been evident since the creation of man. One such example in scriptures of "black magic" is when Moses met with the Egyptian Pharoah to tell him he must free the Israelites who had been enslaved by evil for nearly 400 years.

"Then Pharaoh called in his sorcerers—the magicians of Egypt—and they were able to do the same thing with their magical arts! Their rods became serpents, too! But Aaron's serpent swallowed their serpents!" (Exodus 7:11-13).

God always overcomes evil with good. Although battles are sometimes lost, God wins the war. Evil also counterfeits the power of God, so if witch doctors are raising the dead in places where demonic spirits rule, we know that everything they do is a counterfeit of everything God can do, including the power of God to raise the dead.

I do not remember an Easter message that included the "walking dead" after Jesus' resurrection, but now I am keenly interested when reading what happened:

"And look! The curtain secluding the Holiest Place in the Temple was split apart from top to bottom; and the earth shook, and rocks broke, and tombs opened, and many godly men and women who had died came back to life again.

130

*After Jesus' resurrection, they left the cemetery and went into Jerusalem,
and appeared to many people there"* (Matthew 27:51-53).

While I never watch horror movies, I've seen momentary images in commercials of scary characters eerily walking around who came alive after death. It's the opposite for all the "walking dead" in the Bible, who are never described as scary zombies. Nowhere in Scripture indicates they had a terrifying presence. I envision them as being full of light and beauty and obviously recognizable in looking just as they had before they died. I don't know whether they were walking in glorified "superpower" bodies, or somehow they were restored to resurrected physical mortal bodies; I just know that life after death and walking again on earth are definitely possible and have happened a lot more than we know about.

Just as the intent of those resurrected after Jesus rose from the grave was to share the need of salvation and eternal life through Jesus Christ, so, too, the miracle story of my life and all who have experienced such a rare miracle must be to remind people to trust in Jesus for eternal life in Heaven, and to realize there is purpose and meaning in all of our lives.

Just as those "walking dead" in the Bible inspired hope in hopeless times, so do testimonies of the ones who, like me, have been resurrected temporarily bring hope for us in this world with so much hopelessness.

Growing up more than 60 years ago in Ohio, the most impressionable item in my childhood was a "glitter" picture (one on which words are written with glue and glitter on cardboard and framed) hung in a most prominent location in my home so we could see it many times a day. Now those words are more meaningful then ever: "Only one life will soon be past, only what's done for Christ will last." (*Only One Life©*, C. T. Studd, 1860-1931)

Before Mr. Studd made popular this profound phrase in his poem, he was a wealthy and famous cricket player. Everyone was surprised when they learned he had used his wealth to invest in God's purpose for his life. What he chose to do with his wealth gave him more pleasure, satisfaction and purpose on earth than anything this world had to offer, and his eternal rewards are far more than we can imagine. He joyfully served as a noted missionary to Africa, China, and India. He also wrote: 'If Jesus Christ be God and died for me, then no sacrifice can be too great for me to make for Him."

Now, many decades later, that glitter picture is a reminder that one primary purpose of my miracle is to encourage anyone who hears of it that all lives matter and what we do with our lives matters most.

No matter who we are or where we live or how old or how young, we matter to God. We have a purpose to live, and not die *before* we are dead.

∞ ∞ ∞

Jesus possessed the power to raise others from the dead even before He gave His life for us on the cross. We are to be as Jesus in this world, so why can't we also have power to raise the dead? I think that Melody did have such power flowing through her fist when she was pounding on my chest. She initiated enough resurrection power to sustain me for as long as it would take. I am also convinced that her prayers and the prayers of others gave resurrection power to doctors and nurses to bring me back to life.

No one can explain the science of how resurrections happened in Bible times, and neither can science and the finite understanding of man explain how it can happen in our modern civilized society. Miracles are not based upon the flawed conclusions of human understanding. The awesome power of God is beyond the limitations of human intellect.

Because of my own heart miracle, I am inclined to believe that God has done profoundly more of the impossible in modern history than we hear or know about. Perhaps it's just not talked about, not only because it seems to be so rare, but also because it's just too unbelievable. Resurrection miracles are the most amazing of all miracles because they are evidence of how earthly death is not final.

Sometimes our sophisticated, proud, civilized culture encourages greater reliance on what man can do, rather than on the infinite wisdom and power of the One who created man. The way some intelligent scholars react to God reminds me of a child who thinks they know better than their parents.

Resurrection miracles require a trust in God like a child who has faith in their parents to know and do what is best. Children are born with a natural spirit of awe and wonder and trust in their Creator and are drawn to know the Lord, which is why most people who give their hearts to Jesus as their Lord and Savior do so before they become adults.

"I tell you the truth. You must change and become like little children. If you don't do this, you will never enter the kingdom of heaven" (Matthew 18:3).

It was when I was a child that I learned to trust in the Lord with all my heart and chose as my "life verse" Proverbs 3:5-6 in the King James Version of the Bible: *"Trust in the Lord with all thine heart and lean not until thine own understanding; in all thy ways, acknowledge Him and He shall direct thy paths"* (Proverbs 3:5-6 KJV).

After more than 60 years of trusting in the Lord with all my heart, I wonder if it helped to prepare my heart to come back to life even though it was once dead. I have no doubt that a lifetime of trusting in the Lord with all my heart has supernaturally charged and healed my heart to live now.

The vast majority of born again believers will begin new life in Heaven when their bodies fail them on earth and they will not reenter mortal flesh. Though we don't understand why or how God chooses to return a soul into their earthly body for a little longer in this world, there is a consensus that when it happens it means God is not finished with the earthly purpose for those He resurrects. It also means there are blessings for those who witness someone who temporarily dies and there are blessings for those who merely hear about NDEs.

A NDE miracle proves that we are all immortally mortal in knowing that God determines the days of our lives. It also confirms that we are not to die before we're dead. We are to live to know and embrace His ordained destiny for our lives. None of us are "accidents." We were purposely created with opportunity for abundant life now and to live in such a way that we build up eternal treasures that will never die.

Believe it or not, God really does raise people from the dead. He did raise me from the dead on April 23, 2022.

Chapter 14

HEAVEN ON MY MIND

"Let not your heart be troubled; you believe in God, believe also in Me. In My Father's house are many mansions; if it were not so, I would have told you. I go to prepare a place for you. And if I go and prepare a place for you, I will come again and receive you to Myself; that where I am, there you may be also. And where I go you know, and the way you know."
Thomas said to Him, 'Lord, we do not know where You are going, and how can we know the way?' Jesus said to him, 'I am the way, the truth, and the life. No one comes to the Father except through Me'" (John 14:1-6 NKJV).

B efore I died and came back to life, I assumed that if I was ever blessed with such a miracle, I would have the best of life on earth after a celestial journey, and tell "everyone" through a book (or any means possible) about my out-of-body adventure to the ultimate "magic kingdom." Perhaps I would have been able to testify of golden streets so pure that light penetrates through them with such brilliance it seems as if you're walking on sunshine. I imagined being able to confirm that in Heaven, "happily ever after" is no longer a fantasy but an eternal reality. I could have possibly shared descriptions of massive pearly gates that opened to see those I'd known and loved on earth awaiting to embrace me with enthusiastic anticipation in an atmosphere permeated with rejuvenating crystals of love. And I would be introduced to distant ancestors who had been praying for me and hug my child who was never born on earth.

My Heaven journey most certainly would have given me opportunity to reassure and comfort those whose pets were a vital part of their lives that they were awaiting them there. I would share how Happy, Karly, Kiwi, Angel, my first dog George, as well as all my kitty children, including Krisy Kreme and Suzi surrounded me with wagging tails and unbridled excitement to see me again, and how they could actually talk!

I can only imagine that if I had remembered witnessing Heaven, that I would tell of how the breath of life there is to inhale joy which travels to every element of your soul and minute particle of your glorified body. I would tell how in Heaven the best of all music ever experienced on earth infuses joy and beauty in every movement and activity and even the flowers sing. And I would tell of witnessing an unlimited spectrum of colors illuminating a perfectly balanced beauty surrounded by homes with inspirational ambiance that uniquely fulfilled the delights of every resident with the comforting joy of finally being home.

Most of all, if I had remembered Heaven in those 39 minutes outside my body on earth, all the remainder of my days when returning would be dedicated to share what Jesus and I talked about, as He would have most definitely shared at least a miniscule amount of crucial insight into the mysteries of life on earth.

To have witnessed the afterlife as portrayed in movies would have confirmed the most wonderful purpose I was to fulfill until the end of my earthly days. At the very least, it would have been such fun and so reassuring if Jesus would have given me a list of exactly what He wanted me to do, where I was to go and when, how I would have the resources to do what He wanted me to do, and how He would provide a "cotton candy car" (similar to Rachel's) to make it possible to be everywhere He wanted me to be. Jesus could have told me when and how all the hearts' desires of my children and grandchildren would be fulfilled, and specifics about how God would continue to use me in their lives to bless them. Oh how good I thought it would have been to have my mind infused with all the answers to the meanings of puzzling Biblical stories and parables that sometimes are so challenging to fully understand. Even to have gained clarity about UFOs, Nephilim, giants, angels, demons, dragons, dinosaurs, and exactly how to live in these "last days" would have been quite helpful.

While I did not need to know about any of the deep perplexities of history and life in general, I thought that just a miniscule amount of insight and wisdom directly from Jesus about what I should and should not do would have been the minimum of what could have been experienced when I was absent from my body and present with the Lord as the Bible assures us in II Corinthians 5:8-9.

Also, since I would be returning to a tired, beaten, bruised, battered and old physical body in a fallen and painful world, wouldn't it have been the greatest help to live without any more physical struggles? Wouldn't it have been useful to receive exact instructions as to how God wanted me to live and help me serve a better purpose as an inspiring testimony in this fallen world where we are not to just survive, but to thrive? I felt it would have been especially helpful to finish the work God had for me on earth if I could have returned to earth as a "Super Senior Avenger" with even just a few superpowers to be able to sustain the "vital and green" and "flourishing like palm trees" life promised to the "righteous" in Psalm 92 for those who were in "old age."

When I was absent from my body, I can only recall two angels assigned to be with me on that brief journey through the shadow of the valley of death. Their only communication about all that was happening was, "All is well." I cannot remember seeing any glorious beauties of my eternal Home, nor being reunited with people and pets I had loved. I was not to consciously remember any inspiring conversations with my beloved Savior, or clear instructions for the rest of my life or for my family. I received no profound understanding of the past, no eternal wisdom about the future of any person or nation, nor even any specific way to engage in my best life now.

Out of the tens of thousands of people who die every day from sudden cardiac arrest, only a very small percentage are revived to live until hospital discharge. But there is an even smaller percentage of survivors who report seeing glorious and/or frightening visions when they "flew away" into the "afterlife." Why? That's something we can ask God one day. I think it might have to do with the blessing for those who have not seen yet believe as Jesus reminded Thomas in John 20:29: *"Then Jesus told him, 'You believe because you have seen me. But blessed are those who haven't seen me and believe anyway.'"*

Since the vast majority of those who have been clinically dead and revived do not remember seeing anything, it is a reasonable assumption that God desires for us to realize the greatest of blessings when believing without seeing. While it is important to be fully aware of life after death, we do not need to know more than what the Bible already tells us about Heaven. Being "Heavenly minded" inspires us to be of more "earthly good," but to know too many specific details of the magnificence of Heaven could make us want to go there before our mission on earth is complete. If you are reading this book, you definitely still have a lot of living to do on earth. And the more you live for Christ on earth, the greater your treasures and joy will be when you get there.

We do not have to see the beauties of Heaven to know Heaven is for real. Enough details are given to us in the scriptures of the reality of our celestial home, including Jesus' promises in John 14:1-6. In Revelation 21-22 we are given inspiring glimpses of the City of God:

"It shone with the glory of God and sparkled like a precious stone—like jasper as clear as crystal. The city wall was broad and high, with twelve gates guarded by twelve angels. And the names of the twelve tribes of Israel were written on the gates. There were three gates on each side—east, north, south, and west. The wall of the city had twelve foundation stones, and on them were written the names of the twelve apostles of the Lamb......

"The wall was made of jasper, and the city was pure gold, as clear as glass. The wall of the city was built on foundation stones inlaid with twelve precious stones: the first was jasper, the second sapphire, the third agate, the fourth emerald, the fifth onyx, the sixth carnelian, the seventh chrysolite, the eighth beryl, the ninth topaz, the tenth chrysoprase, the eleventh jacinth, the twelfth amethyst. The twelve gates were made of pearls—each gate from a single pearl! And the main street was pure gold, as clear as glass.

"I saw no temple in the city, for the Lord God Almighty and the Lamb are its temple. And the city has no need of sun or moon, for the glory of God illuminates the city, and the Lamb is its light. ...Its gates will never be closed at the end of day because there is no night there. And all the nations will bring their glory and honor into the city. Nothing evil will be allowed to enter, nor anyone who practices shameful idolatry and dishonesty—but only those whose names are written in the Lamb's Book of Life.

"Then the angel showed me a river with the water of life, clear as crystal, flowing from the throne of God and of the Lamb. It flowed down the center of the main street. On each side of the river grew a tree of life, bearing twelve crops of fruit, with a fresh crop each month. The leaves were used for medicine to heal the nations.

"No longer will there be a curse upon anything. ....And there will be no night there—no need for lamps or sun—for the Lord God will shine on them. And they will reign forever and ever."

We do not need to have a conversation with Jesus to learn how to live a victorious and abundant life on earth. He has written all the instructions we need in the Bible books of Matthew, Mark, Luke and John, Ephesians, Philippians, Proverbs, I Thessalonians and throughout all Scripture, through accounts of real people going through real challenges. Instructions as to what we are to do and how we are to live are in other Biblical passages such as:

"Trust in the Lord with all your heart; do not depend on your own understanding. Seek his will in all you do, and he will show you which path to take" (Proverbs 3:5-6).

"Always be joyful. Never stop praying. Be thankful in all circumstances, for this is God's will for you who belong to Christ Jesus. Do not stifle the Holy Spirit. Do not scoff at prophecies, but test everything that is said. Hold on to what is good. Stay away from every kind of evil" (I Thessalonians 5:16-22 NLT).

The truth is, we already have superpowers far greater than any fantasy character. And we don't need a magic wand or elixir to experience supernatural blessings and joy. We learn about our superpowers in the Bible and activate them when we pray:

"Call to Me and I will answer you, and tell you [and even show you] great and mighty things, [things which have been confined and hidden], which you do not know and understand and cannot distinguish" (Jeremiah 33:3, AMP).

The unlimited power of the Holy Spirit lives in you when Jesus becomes your Lord and Savior.

"I pray that from His glorious, unlimited resources, he will empower you with inner strength through his Spirit. Then Christ will make his home in your hearts as you trust in him. Your roots will grow down into God's love and keep you strong. And may you have the power to understand, as all God's people should, how wide, how long, how high, and how deep his love is" (Ephesians 3:16-19, NLT).

With the Holy Spirit in you, you are a "spiritual avenger" with powers to conquer evil and be victorious because of your access to the ultimate superpowers from the Throne of Heaven. You don't have to die physically on earth first be filled with Heavenly powers, but you do need to be born again spiritually. With Christ Jesus at home in your heart, all your powers are fueled by His Love. What greater power could we be promised than to have the power for abundant life on earth and the hope of Heaven?

Even though I was not blessed with visions and messages I thought I needed from Jesus, I was blessed with a miracle and message of hope that God knew I needed to fulfill His purposes. To be a walking miracle is a message of the unlimited power of God and gives great glory to God, which is far more significant than merely understanding better all the mysteries of life and the universe. Frankly, it would have been such fun to share details of Heaven, but there already are lots of people who are doing a really good job talking about their NDEs. There are never enough encouraging testimonies about how to live victoriously on earth until we all get to Heaven. We need help to be and become the best God created us to be. We need to know we have a purpose to keep going when it seems as if our "get up and go" has "got up and went." When we are hurting, lonely, discouraged, rejected, we need reassurance that God loves us, God likes us, and He has a wonderful plan for our lives. It is never hopeless when we hope in God.

My miraculous testimony is proof that with God, *all* things *are* possible to anyone, anywhere who believes in Him. It doesn't matter if you are rich, poor, old, young, men, women, boys, girls single, married, happy or sad, successful or a failure, sick or healthy, a celebrity or someone nobody knows, you are a walking miracle as a child of God. Every day you can live with a glorious purpose that will bless you forever in Heaven and all eternity. You don't have to experience a miracle of coming back from the dead as I did to make a miraculous difference in the way you live your life every day and for all the days of your life.

My primary message after having returned to life after death is to know that what we do and do not do in this world has eternal consequences. Everything I've shared in this book can be summed up in two simple sentences:

1) Live until you die.

2) Don't die before you're dead.

Confused? You might be asking; *if we are still alive each day in this world, how can we die before we are dead? It doesn't seem to make any sense.* It means that life is for living and as long as we live, we are not to waste our lives by merely existing. It is possible to just be "going through the motions of life," but not really living as God created your life to be. No matter what, no matter how hard or hopeless it may seem, if you are still living and your heart is still beating, then you can still have a life worth living. We should all strive to be walking "miracles" and not walking zombies. The "why" can be a long list of reasons, or it can be a very short explanation. The Apostle Paul said it best:

"For to me, to live is Christ and to die is gain" (Philippians 1:21, NLT).

Paul had every reason to give up, but even when he was stoned and left for dead, he still would not die before he was dead. After being stoned and left for dead, Paul had an out-of-body experience in which he saw Heaven. Paul knew of the glories awaiting us there that we can only imagine. However, when returning to his earthly mission, he did not desire to go to his Heavenly home until he *finished* his work on earth. If he had decided life was too hard to keep living on earth, he never would have written 13 books in the New Testament about salvation through Jesus Christ and the way to live with joy and victory over evil. His choice to not die before he was dead has blessed multiplied millions with hope and inspiration to live for Christ throughout the world for the last 2000 years.

For me, no matter how deep my longing and passion to participate in the lives of my grandsons and encourage them to know, love and serve the Lord and be and become all that God has created them to be; no matter how much my heart wanted to rejoice with my adult children to be blessed with all the desires of their hearts they have yet to realize, and no matter how much I still wanted to enjoy working as a model and actress and wedding officiant and having more delightful lunches with Claire, nothing in my life was enough to keep me from begging and pleading with God to not send me back on earth if I had that choice. I didn't even have dogs anymore and precious time with my grandsons had become less available to me.

Therefore, If I would have recalled seeing Heaven, I would have begged and pleaded with God to not send me back to earth! I do not have anything close to the best in this world, so I have many reasons to prefer Heaven instead of struggling down here any longer.

So why did Paul, who had suffered more than any of us can imagine, have the strength to finish the work God had for him on earth? It was because of what he learned from his personal experience of the afterlife, of Heaven. No doubt, he must have wanted to stay in Heaven, but because God desired for him to complete his purpose on earth, God used him to bless millions through the centuries with his instructions on how to know joy, peace, purpose, and be victorious in and through all things. It was after having witnessed Heaven that he was able to sing and write about joy, even in prison.

I did not have to see Heaven to realize that the rest of my life is to be the best of my life. God alone understands what I've been through on earth that would have caused me to beg to never come back here. God alone is who I trust to help me fulfill His ordained destiny for my life. I know Heaven is for real, but I also know there is a purposeful, fulfilling, rewarding plan for the rest of my life on earth that will make Heaven even more wonderful than anything I could have seen, heard or experience through a NDE.

Even though we do not have a NDE like Paul, we learn from him about Heaven. And the more Heavenly minded we are, the more earthly good we become. We should have Heaven on our minds all the time. For to see our lives through Heaven's eyes is to see our purpose for truly living until we die.

I often used to sing solos in church services when I was just a child and teenager. All of my favorite songs were those with lyrics about Heaven, such as: "Heaven came down and glory filled my soul," and "Heaven is a wonderful place, filled with glory and grace, I want to see my Savior's face, Heaven is a wonderful place," and "This world is not my home, I'm just a passin' through, my treasures are laid up somewhere beyond the blue, the angels beckon me from Heaven's open door, and I can't be at home in this world anymore."

My favorite Heaven hymn was *When we all get to Heaven©*.

> Sing the wondrous love of Jesus, sing his mercy and His grace; In the mansions bright and blessed, He'll prepare for us a place.
> When we all, get to Heaven, what a day of rejoicing that will be, When we all see Jesus, we'll sing and shout the victory....
> Let us then be true and faithful, trusting, serving every day; Just one glimpse of Him in glory, Will the tolls of life repay...
> When we all, get to Heaven, what a day of rejoicing that will be; When we all see Jesus, we'll sing and shout the victory....
> Onward to the prize before us! Soon His beauty we'll behold; Soon the pearly gates will open, We shall tread the streets of gold..." (Eliza E Hewitt, 1851-1920; Emily D Wilson 1865-1942)

During the years I was active in full time music ministry, I was often asked to sing this hymn and many other Heaven songs, such as *Beyond the Sunset©* at funerals (which I always refer to as Celebrations of Life). And I can't hear the song *I Can Only Imagine©* by Mercy Me without weeping tears of joy.

I absolutely, most certainly, sure do long for Heaven every day, and all that is awaiting me in Heaven. Carson has told me since I died that he knew if I died it would be OK because he knew I would be in Heaven with Happy and Karly. I reminded him that I needed more time on earth to "finish the race."

I do not want my life to be over until it is really *over!* For me, it's sometimes been "slow going" doing all I want and need to do, especially in recent years. God gave me more time. God has given you more time. God's amazing grace gave the cherished blessing of opportunity to finish the race He has called me to win, and I want the prize!

"I strain to reach the end of the race and receive the prize for which God is calling us up to heaven because of what Christ Jesus did for us" (Philippians 3:14).

"Therefore, since we are surrounded by such a huge crowd of witnesses to the life of faith, let us strip off every weight that slows us down, especially the sin that so easily trips us up. And let us run with endurance the race God has set before us" (Hebrews 12:1, NLT).

It's worth repeating: Heaven was, is and always needs to be on my mind, your mind, and on the mind of every believer in Jesus Christ as their Savior.

Even before I died I felt as if I had already done my best: taken care of my parents, family, children, husband, grandchildren and others; given my best at any task whether I liked it or not; did not repay "evil for evil;" cast my cares on the Lord; prayed all the time; rejoiced all the time, and gave thanks all the time. Even though I felt I was no longer wanted nor needed in this world, God still had more for me to do in my earthly abode before I went to my Heavenly home.

Since God brought me back to earth, I know that I have yet to experience the best to come for me here. My race is not over. Even though I feel as if a granny like me living in a borrowed Florida condo is the most unlikely person that God would choose to inspire hope to anyone, I have been/am constantly reminded that God often uses the least to fulfill His great purposes.

No greater example is given to us than every Christmas season when we are reminded that Jesus came to earth in the most lowly position. He was not born into a life of royalty, even though He was the King of Kings. His birth was in stinky stable (or cave) surrounded by animals and witnessed by lowly shepherds. Yet wealthy and influential wise men sought to see Him, even as a child. He was born the least among humanity, but had the greatest purpose.

If God can use a "talking donkey" to save His people from death (read about it in Numbers 22), then He of course can use a "Resurrected-from-the-dead-angel-seeing-granny" to help inspire hope in a world where hopelessness abounds. So, while I know without a doubt that the "best" of TBIYTC (my joyism of The Best Is Yet To Come) is ultimately in Heaven, I know also that the best for trusting in the Lord with all our hearts on earth is yet to come!

∞ ∞ ∞

A year after my husband went to Heaven, I flew to a conference about Heaven led by Randy Alcorn at the Billy Graham Training Center, The Cove, in the mountains outside of Asheville, North Carolina. I arrived on the first anniversary of my husband's death. While I was driving up to the beautifully inspirational location, I witnessed a sunset so amazing it looked as if it were a portal to Heaven. I began to weep and pulled onto the side of the road to gain my composure. As I stopped, the radio began playing a song I'd never heard before. When listening to the lyrics, my weeping turned to tears streaming down my face as I listened to a man whose voice sounded much like my husband's beautiful singing voice.

If You Could See me Now©
Our prayers have all been answered
I finally arrived
The healing that had been delayed
Is now realized
No one's in a hurry
There's no schedule to keep
We're all enjoying Jesus
Just sitting at His feet

If you could see me now
I'm walking streets of gold
If you could see me now
I'm standing tall and whole
If you could see me now
You'd know I've seen His face

If you could see me now
You'd know the pain's erased
You wouldn't want me
To ever leave this place
If only you could see me now

My light and temporary trials
Have worked out for my good
To know it brought Him glory
When I misunderstood
Though we've had our sorrows
They can never compare
To what Jesus has in store for us
No language can share" (Don Moen, 1950 -)

The "portal to Heaven" sunset and the "coincidental" song on the radio, were gifts from God to my heart and prepared me for the blessings of Randy Alcorn's Eternal Perspective ministry teachings. I had never heard of Alcorn before then. I was there after searching for a beautiful place to go and spend some time crying out to God. The Cove was the perfect location, an oasis of peace and beauty. When Randy just happened to be there for "Heaven Talk," I knew it was where I was supposed to be.

What I gleaned from those days filled with Biblical inspiration was to serve as a foundation for Heaven-minded living for the rest of my life. I purchased multiple copies of all his books to distribute on my chaplain visits. At that time, Alcorn was best known for his novels, *Deadline*© (Multnomah, 2006) and *Safely Home*© (Tyndale House, 2011), which are two of the best books I have ever read. In more recent years, he is known for the best seller, *Heaven*© (Tyndale House, 2004), which I also enjoy giving to others -as well as *Heaven For Children*© that I just gave to my grandsons. His writings encourage us to know the blessings of living from an eternal perspective.

Our decisions matter most when we make them through what would matter most if we could see our lives from Heaven's perspective. We already have an eternal life – but how we will live for the rest of our eternal life is dependent upon how we live now in the few years remaining during this part of our eternal life on earth.

Since I died, my grandson Gavin has told me about a dream he had of my Heavenly home. I listened in awe and wonder as he described my celestial destination in detail similar to a dream my son Daniel had shared with me when I was dealing with overwhelming challenges.

I had never before told Gavin about Daniel's dream.

This is Daniel's edited letter dated October 25, 2011, before Gavin was even born:

MOM JOY'S HEAVENLY ABODE

Dreamt by Daniel Timothy

> I ascended a staircase to an upstairs portion of your dwelling. When I reached the main room it was very large and elegant. It had a wraparound couch made of plush red material. The windows were huge and made of such clear crystals that you could barely tell they were there unless they sparkled. The view was of endless beauty... I mentioned that 30 foot ceilings, a great view and lots of windows were plenty to be happy about, but just to make sure, I suggested we go to check out the neighborhood. We went downstairs and out onto the street. The entire area was very active and filled with beautiful architecture, the atmosphere was delightful. Directly across the street from your dwelling was a town dedicated to celebrating Christmas. It seemed like a wonderful place!
>
> Remember when you're down and out because of this crappy world, this and so much more awaits you.
>
> TBIYTC.

I know God sometimes speaks through dreams. God used the dreams of my son and grandson to remind me how, even though I often feel homeless on earth, it's because I am just not home yet. The home Daniel and Gavin described is exactly what I love and I've no doubt that God has prepared such a place for me. Through my son's and grandson's dreams, God was reminding me of His love and that I was not forgotten. I am blessed to be a blessing, and I am reminded of how much I need to be more Heavenly minded than I am. The more Heavenly minded I am, the more earthly good I will be.

While I still would prefer a more comfortable life of ease on earth, when I think of Heaven, I am reminded that it is never easy to do what is best. I know the greatest comfort until I'm Home is in the comforter – the Holy Spirit – who dwells in the inner chamber of my heart: "...*we are able to hold our head high no matter what happens and know that all is well, for we know how dearly God loves us, and we feel this warm love everywhere within us because God has given us the Holy Spirit to fill our hearts with his love*" (Romans 5:5).

My heart may sometimes be troubled, but I have persistent joy in my heart, for I know the best is yet to come. TBIYTC!

"...no mere man has ever seen, heard, or even imagined what wonderful things God has ready for those who love the Lord" (I Corinthians 2:9).

"Let not your heart be troubled. You are trusting God, now trust in me. There are many homes up there where my Father lives, and I am going to prepare them for your coming. When everything is ready, then I will come and get you, so that you can always be with me where I am" (John 14:1-3).

Chapter 15

ACHY-BREAKY HEART

"But take heed to yourselves, lest your hearts be weighed down with ...the cares of this life...." (Luke 21:34 KJV).

"Though You have made me see troubles, many and bitter, You will restore my life again; from the depths of the earth, You will bring me up again" (Psalm 71:20).

"He heals the broken hearted and binds up their wounds" (Psalm 147:3).

Life hurts. When life hurts, your heart hurts. When you hurt, your heart aches. When your heart aches too long, it can become an *achy-breaky heart*. This phenomenon is not just the title of a catchy country song, but it is a reality that can have devastating consequences.

The word "heart" occurs 862 times in both the Old and New Testaments of the Bible. If God's Word is filled with revelations of matters of the heart, then our hearts matter. Our hearts are awesome and powerful beyond what we are consciously aware of or can imagine.

"Guard your heart above all else, for it determines the course of your life"
(Proverbs 4:23, NLT).

"For as a man thinks in his heart, so is he" (Proverbs 23:7, NKJV).

The Hebrew word for heart and its meaning in this context are *leb*, and "keep above all keepings." Your heart is the keeper of all things. An "achy-breaky" heart can break every part of your life, physically, mentally, and spiritually. So, it is important to do everything possible to guard our hearts from harm, beginning with our thoughts. For what we think can cause the "keeper" of all things within us to keep beating, or not. And that is why MHMs must fill our days; that is why we must think on good things (Philippians 4). It is a matter of life and death:

"A cheerful heart does good like medicine, but a broken spirit makes one sick"
(Proverbs 17:22).

"Heart Healthy" is not just in reference to a list of foods and supplements that are proven to benefit your physical heart, it also includes nourishment of our spirit and soul. Food and medicines are of some benefit for heart health, but the Bible offers the best prescriptions for how our heart can function to give us abundant life which goes far beyond mere physical nourishment and care. Unlike the negative side effects of certain foods or meds, the only consequences of what I referred to in the MHM chapter as "joy pills" are to empower us to enjoy life to the fullest as God has created it to be; to find a way when there seems to be no way; to protect us from all that is in this world that causes an "achy-breaky" heart, and to thrive when merely surviving seems impossible.

Consuming the Word of God regarding matters of the heart matters to all dimensions of life. Some of my favorite "joy pills" to encourage a healthy heart of joy, peace, love, and faith include:

"Create in me a new, clean heart, O God, filled with clean thoughts and right desires"
(Psalm 51:10).

"You will seek me and find me when you seek me with all your heart. I will be found by you," declares the Lord" (Jeremiah 29:13-14, NIV).

"May he give you the desires of your heart and make all your plans succeed"
(Psalm 20:4, NIV).

"The Lord does not look at the things people look at. People look at the outward appearance, but the Lord looks at the heart" (I Samuel 16:7, NIV).

"Let love and faithfulness never leave you; bind them around your neck, write them on the tablet of your heart. Then you will win favor and a good name in the sight of God and man" (Proverbs 3:3-4, NIV).

"Wherever your treasure is, there the desires of your heart will also be"
(Matthew 6:21, NLT).

"Jesus replied, 'You must love the Lord your God with all your heart, all your soul, and all your mind'" (Matthew 22:37, NLT).

"Take delight in the Lord, and he will give you the desires of your heart"
(Psalm 37:4, NIV).

"Be of good courage, And He shall strengthen your heart, All you who hope in the Lord"
(Psalm 31:24, NKJV).

"Teach us to number our days, that we may gain a heart of wisdom"
(Psalm 90:12, NIV).

There have been numerous studies which starkly revealed how life is dependent upon much more than just meeting physical needs. One disturbing study in 1944 was with 40 newborn babies. Half of these infants were in a special facility where they were only provided with minimal care of feeding and diaper changes. Adults with them were instructed not to even look at or touch the unfortunate babies for anything other than providing a sanitary existence. The other 20 babies were rocked, cuddled, talked to, sung to, and played with, in addition to having their basic needs met. The horrific experiment ended in just four months after all the babies that had not been shown love, died. It was alarming to learn that all those precious children died with healthy bodies, but broken hearts. The official determination of the cause of their deaths was "failure to thrive."

When there is no love, there is no life. This tragic reality was also confirmed through a study of how most institutionalized infants in the United States in the 19th Century died of *marasmus* ("wasting away"). By 1915, surveys of nearly all orphanages reported that most infants under age 2 had died from a "failure to thrive." (Chapin 1915; cited in Montagu 1986, p. 97). In similar studies, it was not just institutionalized babies who suffered from the absence of loving attention, but also babies and children in any environment. Babies thrive through loving interactions of moms, dads, grandparents, siblings, aunts, uncles, friends and others, through play, hugs, laughter, mental stimulation, and emotional concern, through connecting with their hearts through love.

There is no better example of how all of life is felt by the heart than from someone who could not experience life in the usual ways we do. Helen Keller (1880 – 1968) lost her ability to see, hear or speak when she was just 19 months old. How was Helen able to have any kind of life at all? The power of God's loving presence through the nurturing touch of her caretaker, Anne Sullivan, and her parents kept her heart beating with joy and purpose. Love transcended all her "impossible" limitations with such profound results that she became one of history's most notable and remarkable communicators of insight and wisdom. She died just shy of her 88th birthday, yet her legacy lives on today with one of her most famous quotes:

"The best and most beautiful things in life cannot be seen—or even touched—but must be felt with the heart."

It is not only babies and children who suffer heartbreak from loveless days and isolation with little or no human interaction, it can happen to anyone at any age when opportunities to live in a thriving environment of joyful relationships are rare, or just not enough.

Feelings of love and intimacy are heart-healing. Feelings of isolation, loneliness, loss, alienation, separation, and hopelessness can cause our physical hearts to become "achy-breaky." Tragically, if the suffering is prolonged, it can lead to a heart that has exhausted all strength to keep on keeping on.

We flourish in an environment of love and interaction with life and the living. Babies most definitely need to be held, hugged, and engaged in life, but so does everyone. We were created for fellowship, to interact with others, and to enjoy life in such a way that is not possible if we are left totally alone with only food, water, and attention only to our physical needs.

When human interaction is unavailable, heart health and healing can be through the companionship with beloved pets and other animals. Love born in the heart can be shared with all of creation having a beating heart. When isolated from those we love, our hearts can still be blessed when communing with our loving Father through prayer and meditating on His Word. However, it is best when God shows up through the love of a person or a pet.

If no human shows up, and we don't even have a sweet, domesticated animal companion, sometimes God will bless our hearts through wild charming critters, bugs, and birds.

During the first few years after my husband's death, while fighting for my son's life, and with my heart burdened about concerning issues with my daughters, I would take advantage of my Delta® employee travel benefits. I would fly to somewhere beautiful for just a day or two to get away from the chaos and sorrow and cry out to God for help. Often, while emotionally numb from the spiritual warfare, I would just sit and gaze upon the beauty of God's creation when birds would come and surround me. I didn't have any food to draw them near, they just came. I wondered if they were angels God sent to comfort me in my grief.

During those months when I found my MHM bird was watching over me, I discovered a chameleon that enjoyed playing on my flowers and plants. A lizard isn't normally considered a usual type of critter that can bless us with "friendship," but it has a beating heart. This lizard was very cute, funny, and entertaining. Its humorous presence was also very effective at taking my mind off chest pain.

God created humanity for fellowship. Our hearts were created to love and can only function with love. We are to love God with all our hearts and are blessed in knowing how much He loves us, but people and animals were created as "God in the flesh" to help us thrive in our flesh.

While animals are uniquely gifted to bring us indescribable wonder, joy and fun, God created humanity to primarily love and be loved in a human family. Our children share our hearts from the moment their hearts begin to beat just under a mom's heart. There is never an age when our sons and daughters are "too old" that the heart connection is severed. My children were grown, with independent lives of their own, but when they faced major life challenges, my heart ached for them as much as it did when they were kids. Even though we rarely see one another, my heart is always "feeling" their hearts. My heart connection is even greater with my young grandsons. My heart rejoices when they are blessed and it is burdened when they are sick or going through difficult challenges. My heart actually "jumps" with excitement sometimes when I watch Gavin and Carson play tennis, and always when Theodore is singing or dancing.

Obviously, the heart connection Adam had with animals was not all that was needed for a healthy heart. That is why not just man was created, but woman for the man and man for woman.

"Then the Lord God said, 'It is not good for the man to be alone. I will make a helper who is just right for him'" (Genesis 2:18 NLT).

If man is not meant to be alone, neither is a woman, boy or girl. We were created to not just survive, but to thrive through the sharing of our hearts with each other. Our connection to the hearts of people we love, or any beloved creature, keeps our hearts beating more than 35 million times a year.

Very few times in modern history have had the detrimental impact of social isolation and distancing from the joy of life and love more than during the covid pandemic, when young and old alike suffered complications of broken hearts. The heartbreak of lives lost by both the virus and misguided treatments for the virus was magnified when many more died from heartbreaking social isolation. It was cruel for anyone or any government to demand "no human contact." Not only were hugs or contact disallowed, but even expressions of love through a kind smile were prohibited by required masks.

When the joys of life are taken away, when a person is ostracized from dynamic human interaction, there is no emotional fuel left for the heart to keep beating. Existence can be sustained for a while through mere physical care, but real living is only possible when life is shared from one genuine beating heart to another. Neither Siri nor Alexa can become a substitute for what God created us for. No matter how sophisticated any robot may be, it can never have a heart!

All that makes life wonderful is rooted in the heart: salvation, joy, love, goodness, kindness, strength, wisdom, treasures, hope, trust, peace, power, victory, delight, desires, passion, purpose, kindness, goodness, patience, beauty, and more. Our hearts are not merely muscles that meds and cardiac rehab can sufficiently stimulate to pump blood and keep oxygen and nutrients flowing through our bodies. As the "keeper of all things," our hearts are the center of everything physical, spiritual, emotional, and mental. Our hearts are the center of everything we feel; everything we experience; all we do or do not do, and relationships with humans, animals, and all creation (but again, not robots). The choices which give us joy bless our hearts; the choices which are not good hurt our hearts. Is it any wonder why all things in life can determine if our heart keeps beating?

The connection between the heart and mind is reflective of how the spiritual and physical cannot be separated. We can know we have eternal life when we ask Jesus into our hearts. When we are saved through the blood of Jesus Christ, the inner sanctum of our heart is possessed by the Holy Spirit. God lives in our hearts. It is through the spiritual functioning of our hearts that we learn how to live. Every emotion is felt in the heart: fear, love, sorrow, joy, peace, surprise, passion, anger, compassion, empathy, and hope. We must do everything possible to cultivate a healthy heart and avoid an "achy-breaky" heart.

It is vital that our hearts are taken care of with the right foods, water, medicines, exercise, and rest, but our hearts need far more to keep beating.

Spiritual and emotional nourishment is so essential to heart health, so much so that those in places of solitary confinement cannot survive without it.

If our heart is overwhelmed from all that is not right and bad in our personal lives and in the world, and we do not enjoy enough of what is right and good, it can hurt our hearts physically much more than we realize.

When our heart is afflicted with too much stress, sorrow, and emotional pain, we can literally become heartbroken. Achy-breaky hearts, indeed, are not only the result of rejection and pain from a broken relationship, but also are a consequences of this broken world. I know because it has happened to me.

∞ ∞ ∞

Often people with good intentions say, "God doesn't give us more than we can bear," as if there is some magical power in thinking we can bear whatever horrible situation we face in our own power. The belief in our amazing power of "bearing all things" is not in the Bible. It is an insensitive and often hurtful comment usually made by those who have truly never gone through "stuff." It is foolish to think that we have complete control in the midst of despair and insurmountable problems.

God does not give us trouble and pain. He does not allow things which are not good to invade our lives because He knows we can bear it. This false concept is inconsistent with His desire to bless us with "good and perfect gifts" (James 1:17); and how *"He gives all things richly to enjoy"* (I Timothy 6:17-19).

God does promise that He does not allow anything that is more than He can bear. The god of this world is the one responsible for all that is not good in this world: sickness, strife, wars, hate, pain, rejection, loss, lack, hardships, and troubles of every kind. To even think that God is the author of the worst in our fallen world and created us to just "grin and bear it" because we think, "I've got this," or tell each other, "You've got this," is to put our trust and faith in our own mortal power without consideration of the omnipotent power of God to overcome the problems we go through when the enemy (aka god of this world) attacks. We can be of good cheer, not because we can handle it, but because we know God can. Sometimes we are not OK. We can't handle it all. Sometimes "too much" is too much, but nothing is "too much" for God to do for us when we cannot do for ourselves.

"Give your burdens to the Lord, and he will take care of you. He will not permit the godly to slip and fall" (Psalm 55:22 NLT).

"I have told you all this so that you will have peace of heart and mind. Here on earth you will have many trials and sorrows; but cheer up, for I have overcome the world" (John 16:33).

"Let him have all your worries and cares, for he is always thinking about you and watching everything that concerns you" (I Peter 5:7).

I knew all of these promises of God before my heart attack. I have been fully aware of the connection between the heart and spirit nearly all my life, yet I was still susceptible to a broken heart in this broken world. We are not immune to being affected by the things in this world, no matter how much we have studied and faithfully believed in God's promises to take care of us and the world.

Even though before my heart attack I suspected that I certainly did not know everything about the heart-spirit dynamic, I was not aware of just how much what I was going through emotionally was eating away at the functioning of my heart, and gradually diminishing its full physical and mechanical functioning.

It was about a month after I died when I read detailed doctors' reports of all that transpired. Two doctors wrote that I showed signs of *Takotsubo*. I had to research what that meant. Takotsubo is medical terminology for "broken heart syndrome." Takotsubo causes your heart's main blood-pumping chamber to change shape and get larger. This weakens the heart muscle and means it doesn't pump blood as well as it should. It's usually triggered by extreme emotional or physical stress.

The word takotsubo comes from the name of a pot used by Japanese fishermen to trap octopuses. When the left ventricle of the heart changes shape, it develops a narrow neck and a round bottom making it look similar to the octopus trap.

Takotsubo can "trap" our hearts into ultimate death. A broken heart is serious. When a husband or wife dies, sometimes the surviving spouse will die mere days later and is believed to have died of a broken heart. This can also happen when a parent loses a child and after a senior adult living alone loses a beloved pet. Unrelenting stress, serious accidents, natural disasters, and lack of sufficient love and human and/or animal interaction hurt the hearts of babies and seniors just as much as they can men and women of any age.

It's understandable that women, far more than men, can suffer from takotsubo. Men and women react differently to emotionally intense situations. Men are more likely to respond outwardly to relieve frustrations through sports, etc. Women more often internalize stress in ways that pierce the heart. Older women are particularly vulnerable when feeling as if they are no longer needed or wanted after a lifetime of helping and caring for their families and others with all their hearts.

By the time we reach our 60s our hearts have become worn out and weak after having been strong for those we love through decades devoted to living and loving with all our hearts!

Even after a lifetime of trusting in the Lord with all our hearts, no one can fully separate from the things in this world that are heartbreaking. We would not be human if we did not "take to heart" life around us. As we age into our senior years, it is easier to be in denial that it is actually happening. As senior women, our needs are often greater than our strength and resources can accommodate, and since we can sometimes be in a situation over which we have no control, and/or where we are helpless to help ourselves, we choose to internalize our emotions more than recognize the danger of conditions and situations that can damage our hearts.

It is often said that "what doesn't kill you, makes you stronger," but what does not make you stronger, can kill you. If it doesn't kill you, it can still hurt your heart in detrimental ways that can make you feel as if you are dying.

While it is assumed my heart attack was not primarily caused by takotsubo, two doctors were in full agreement that indications of that affliction had negatively affected my heart. Something was obviously not functioning as it should have been because of an "achy-breaky" heart.

Primary causes of heart attacks are: diabetes, illegal drug use, high blood pressure, obesity, smoking and stress. None of these applied to me except stress, lots, and lots of stress. I kept the pain of what I was going through between me and God. It was not good to internalize my grief and stress, but it happened. It was not surprising to have discovered indications of takotsubo in the doctors' reports.

In the years before covid I had already begun to deal with issues of loss of income, broken down cars, major concerns with my adult children, and other issues that were much harder to deal with without a life companion.

I fondly remember how the years before covid were filled with more of a MHM life. Until 2019, I still had Happy and Karly and Kiwi to enjoy heart healthy canine companionship. I had enjoyed Heaven on earth moments with Happy for nearly 17 years. Karly had been my darling doggy daughter for 7. After a few years of being her grandma, Rachel gave her to me and Happy when Gavin was a baby. I also had the joys of caring for my grand-dog Kiwi when Melody lived with me. These precious doggy babies were "God in furry flesh" during the years of navigating life challenges without a human partner while I was growing older. Their presence was one of perpetual joy and a reminder of what life is all about.

For the most part since I had moved to Florida, none of the typical limitations of growing old seemed to matter. I had my Happy, Karly, and Kiwi. I was enjoying frequent opportunities to work as a senior model for commercials and officiating for weddings, baby dedications, and celebration of life ceremonies. My heart was blessed with countless "best days ever" shared with my grandsons. Some of the very best of the best were when Gavin and Carson stayed with me and Happy, Karly, and Kiwi. The walks, the laughter, the love we shared with our furry family were for me the best and most heart healthy years of my life.

My grandsons and dogs filled most days with an abundance of MHM laughter and fun. Funny things always were happening when all the boys and dogs were together, so there was always enough joy in my life to ensure my heart was healthy. One particularly funny incident came to mind recently when I found a poster with Karly pictured as "missing"; it had been printed when she had "disappeared." We all thought that somehow Karly had run out when a repairman had opened the front door. We thoroughly searched the condo, we prayed, we expanded our search throughout the immediate and adjacent neighborhoods, we printed and distributed 100 posters, posted her missing on social media, and called animal control and shelters to learn if someone had found her.

Exasperated, we circled together in the condo to pray. Holding hands and weeping, we earnestly asked for God to bring Karly back to us. Well, when we opened our eyes, Karly was walking out of my closet towards us. We all burst out laughing at how she had managed to hide so well in my closet that none of us could see her, despite searching there at least four times. Perhaps when we prayed, God *had* just transported her there from where she had been.

Things began to change for the worse in April of 2019, when precious Happy took his journey over the "Rainbow Bridge." The grief of losing Happy pierced my heart. Dogs remind us of all that is good and wonderful. Dogs teach us of God's loyalty, faithfulness, and unconditional love. There is a consensus among dog owners that since they are connected to our hearts, dogs often assume the personality of their owners and naturally become our best friends. With such an obvious heart connection with our dogs, they are capable of giving us countless heart healing moments of Heaven on earth, but when they are gone it is unbearably heart breaking. To be disconnected from the 17-year heart connection with Happy caused my heart to physically ache with inconsolable grief. I literally felt "something" in my heart that didn't seem right, an unusual and peculiar physical pain. Perhaps it was an early symptom of takotsubo. After Happy was gone, little by little, many other joys of life were gradually disappearing.

The month before covid, precious Kiwi would join Happy on the other side of the "Rainbow Bridge." In 2020, I saw my grandsons less and less. With my grandsons and Happy and Kiwi out of my life, it was heartbreaking, but Karly's heart healing presence was still with me.

In June 2020, my heart was paralyzed with grief the day Karly suddenly became paralyzed. She had been her usual delightful self and had played with Gavin and Carson the day before she suddenly collapsed. It was two months into the covid lockdowns, when it was often difficult to seek immediate medical care for people and for dogs. Since she could not even stand, let alone walk, and was unable even to bark, I persisted in finding help for her.

Thankfully, I learned of a local dog surgeon who specialized in a phenomenal procedure to save Karly's life. Just the thought of losing Karly after not fully recovering from the deaths of Happy and Kiwi made me feel as if my heart was breaking little by little.

It wasn't just the loss of two of my beloved doggies and near death of another that made my heart feel as if something was just not right, it was the impact of covid upon all of life.

At first, it was not a hardship since the hope was that it was only a temporary concern to deal with and seemed to be an extra nasty cold. However, when the projected "two weeks" of shut downs became another week, then another, things started to change in many ways that were heartbreaking for me individually and for all our society.

My initial response to obstacles was to do what I've always done: find a way to make the negative issues have positive benefits. One way our family faced covid was to keep living, working, and sharing time together. My daughters made deliveries from phone and internet orders when their KYDS children's boutique was forced to close to in-person customers. I was able to do a few weddings for couples who decided to engage in nuptials in their homes after closure of their chosen venues. Just after the covid lockdowns were mandated, we joyfully celebrated Carson's birthday with a few friends playing games and having mask-free, non-social-distancing fun. Rachel and Kevin hosted Easter festivities, including a wonderful dinner and "egg hunt" at their home with our unmasked family and friends.

Before the "covid week" lockdown had been extended to over a month, we had rearranged plans for my big 65th birthday at the Magic Kingdom Castle and Epcot™. When Disney closed, those plans evaporated. When the lockdowns continued, it didn't seem as if I was to have the much anticipated "grand" celebration for that momentous birthday anywhere.

However, Florida's governor DeSantis wisely determined it was time for businesses and restaurants to open up for customers again on my birthday, May 4th. It was a nice "birthday gift" from my governor. We were excited to find an awesome restaurant with the courage to open on that day at a local Town Center where nearly all other stores and restaurants remained closed. We all dressed up in our best outfits. I wore a super sparkly gown to symbolize that the older you get, the more "bright and shining" you can become. All my children, their spouses, Gabi's mom, and all three of my grandsons joined together in feasting and fun. After our absolutely wonderful dinner in the nearly empty restaurant, Kevin and Daniel set up a large speaker on the flatbed of his pickup truck in the large empty parking lot and played jubilant music that we sang loudly and danced to. I felt that my fun and wonderful 65th birthday celebration was so heart healing that I could make it through any challenges ahead.

But after that glorious day celebrating my official entrance into the world of the elderly, the negative impact of covid began to slowly take its toll on my heart. The weddings I had scheduled for the year were gradually being canceled, model jobs were non-existent, and no one was allowed to gather for baby dedications or life celebrations for the survivors of those who died during the pandemic. I had outlived my Delta® pension, so the loss of income was beginning to become a heavy concern upon my heart when all other income fizzled and resources were exhausted.

What began to happen in society was taking its toll on everyone. "No human contact" and "social distancing," forcing everyone to wear masks and the "required" use of unproven treatments causing debilitating side effects were more detrimental to health than the virus itself.

My personal encounters with angry strangers hurt my heart more than I realized. For not wearing a mask, I was told by an angry old man in a coffee shop that I "should die." I thought he was kidding and laughed, but it made him angrier that I did not take him seriously. "At least I am alive," he angrily responded. "Well, so am I also alive-and far more alive than you!" was my not-so-kind response. I couldn't go into a store without an employee or "nazi-type" customer becoming angry and condemning toward me if I was "mask-free."

When Gov. DeSantis encouraged churches to open, I was excited to attend one nearby that dared to do so. However, my "joy bubble" burst when I was escorted out of a church service for non-compliance of the "6 feet rule." Six times I tried to sit where it was considered "safe." But each time, a "covid guard" would eerily approach me and demand I move. When I asked why most in the congregation were sitting close together, the response was that they were families. *Aren't we all in the family of God?* Apparently not. That church should have stayed closed. It was the first time I'd ever been thrown out of church!

When I collapsed in tears in the church lobby, a masked woman approached me at a "safe distance" to tell me the man was "sorry" for what he had done, but they needed to follow "requirements" by the CDC. "He *should* be sorry," I declared through my tears. I reminded her that the CDC was not the law, and our Florida Governor was not sending people to arrest church goers who were not sitting 6 feet apart. I didn't go to any church for a long time after that heart sickening day.

One way I hoped to compensate for my lost income in 2020 was to become a contestant on *Worst Cooks in America*™, fully *expecting* to win $25K. While I've already mentioned my failure to succeed at that hopeful opportunity, it was also stressful to realize the effort had cost me more than the minimal earnings for the performance of trying to win.

The most stressful parts of that adventure were the challenges of flying to and from New York City and living there for a couple of weeks. Traveling on flights felt like being in the twilight zone. Had everyone gone insane? When on the planes, announcements were made every 15 minutes to "stay 6 feet apart" when the flights were totally full, with passengers sitting mere inches from one another. Also, water was not even served because to drink the water would mean masks had to be removed, and masks were to be worn constantly. In NYC, there were a few opportunities to get relief from the madness of stressful covid enforcements which included being called daily by the government to ensure we were in "compliance". At least there were enough MHMs shared with other contestants in the hotel where we were all quarantined. Fellowship with my new and fascinating "worst cook" friends balanced out the stress of being in that restricted covid city. We would gather in my room, which was larger than others and we would enjoy mask-free fun, laughter, get to know each other, and enjoy our meals. Sometimes we would meet for a break from it all on the roof, once to have a mini birthday party. A couple times, we snuck out of the hotel and found a few shops that had dared to open, but the NYC covid restrictions were "heart hurting" at a time when my heart was already taking in worse than the good could handle.

∞ ∞ ∞

By His grace, God opened a door of balancing out the bad of NYC with the good of Jacksonville through an opportunity to film an episode of a new fun HGTV™ series. A production crew spent several days headquartered in my condo to film an episode entitled "Melody" for a new series, *40-Year-Old Property Virgin*© about those nearly 40 buying their first homes. Melody had saved enough to do so through diligently working and living with me a few years. It was such fun filming the shoot with the best and most amazing producers, directors, and camera crew. The premise of the series was an unusual take on the popular *House Hunters*© series on the same channel. They not only hired Melody as the "star", but Rachel and I, Gavin, Carson, and even Karly were the "co-stars." The "on demand" episode featured a photo of Melody and me, whom she described as her "hilarious Mom." Filming for the show was during Thanksgiving month 2020. The joys we shared in working together for that production had magnified our gratitude of what God had done to bless us through the challenges and losses that year. The greatest blessings were in how we loved, supported and cared for one another and grew to live more by faith and not fear.

It is ironic and humorous that some of the most unusual and fun opportunities for me during that chaotic "covid year," were to be cast on programs for two of my favorite televised networks. While it would have been even more amazing to also have had the opportunity to join the cast for a movie on my other favorite Hallmark™ channel, merely acting in two very interesting productions for HGTV™ and Food Network™ was not only encouraging to my heart, but perhaps encouraging to others over 65 who had grown discouraged during covid, and who needed a reminder that they were not too old. Life had *not* passed them by and they could choose to replace fear with faith that they could, indeed, escape from their condos and do something fun and unusually adventurous. If I could do it, any senior can.

The filming of the program, my 65th birthday, family birthday and holiday celebrations, Gavin, and Carson trips together, joyful days with Theodore, Karly's miraculous recovery, were such welcome and wonderful merry heart times of 2020 that I was confident my heart had sufficiently been given enough "merry heart medicine" to be healthy and happy enough to handle all the other stress of the pandemic successfully. It most certainly was enough temporary relief from the unusual aching of my heart that I had begun to regularly feel from the consequences of covid.

However, not long after the heart healing fun, other attempts to live a normal life in an abnormal world became more and more challenging.

Our annual trips to Disney and SeaWorld Christmas celebrations were stressful when strangers would rebuke Gavin and Carson for not wearing their masks "properly" when they fell below their noses. People walked around fearful that they would get infected by others if accidentally coming within less than 6 feet. Some actually reminded me of "zombies." But what we missed most at our favorite Florida destinations were the glorious and beautiful Christmas concerts and celebrations that were curtailed or canceled during the covid restrictions.

By 2021, heart hurting life events were becoming more and more frequent. Early that year, I had to have MOHS surgery to remove skin cancer on my nose. A nurse angrily refused to let me walk in the hallway without a mask over my bandaged nose and I had to yell for the doctor to let me out. While some couples began to reschedule their weddings canceled in 2020, many couples did not remain together and many venues still remained closed. I was able to do only a few weddings that year. My greatest heart healing moments were days with my grandsons, but even those were less frequent than all the years before. At least I loved every moment of having Karly with me every day. I was thankful to officiate one life celebration ceremony that relatives insisted on arranging in spite of the challenges in doing so. Circumstances surrounding covid were causing broken hearts everywhere and to everyone. There was too much death, not just from the virus, but from all things related to it.

I thought I was being given another chance in August 2021 to win some much-needed income on a new TV game show competition that I failed to do on another TV "worst" show. I was selected to be a contestant on Jay Leno's *You Bet Your Life*©. The flights were booked, the shoot date confirmed, but the evening before I was to board my flight, tests confirmed I had covid. I had remained covid free for a year and a half. Of all times to get it, on an extremely rare day, a once in a lifetime day of a great and fun opportunity. I guess you could say that 8 months after that failed opportunity I was to get another chance at the ultimate game of "you bet your life." And boy, oh boy, did I "hit the jackpot."

I did get very sick with covid that one and only time I would get it. I know it helped to have a doctor immediately find a pharmacy that would fill a prescription for proven remedies of Ivermectin and hydroxychloroquine which most places would not carry. Also, I fortified my system with covid-busting supplements such as zinc and vitamin C which I had learned about through personal research and my brave Dr. Cappasso's recommendations. Fortunately, De Santis also had just opened up Regeneron clinics where I was infused with lifesaving treatment the very day I was to be in California, meeting Jay Leno, and earning some much needed income doing something that would also have been a lot of much needed fun.

We all did our best to focus on the blessings during the continued covid complications and restrictions throughout 2021. We shared the best

Thanksgiving celebration ever at the Crismond house when, for the first time, all my children and grandchildren were together on that most loved holiday. They had also invited some local college tennis players who were from several other countries to join us for the best time of feasting, trivia fun, and MHM fellowship, even a "ping-pong" tournament.

By early 2022, so much had gone wrong and very little right that my life seemed as if it had become too much for my heart to bear. I didn't realize how much I was so discouraged before the heart attack until months after, when I had written in my journal I felt as if I were dying.

One of the very the best blessings during those disparaging covid years was how my best friend, Claire, always knew when to call and invite me to what we both referred to as our CJ/JC therapy lunches. When we were able to ventilate our sorrows and share our joys at those wonderful MHM lunches, usually at restaurants overlooking the intercoastal or the ocean, we were getting the best medicine to continue battling through all the craziness of the covid world.

In spite of so much good to rejoice in during those not-so-good years, I knew something was wrong with me, but refused to consider just how wrong it could be. There had just been too many heart hurting months and not enough days of heart healing.

Between those lifesaving CJ/JC lunches and few most joyful days with my grandsons and other blessed times, I continued to feel weird "gurgling" sensations in my chest that I dismissed as indigestion. While assuming it was nothing, there was still a small voice inside me that urged me to purchase an herbal heart healing supplement. The insert in the package said, "Get ready to feel your best ever." Well, perhaps they meant to feel the best in Heaven because it was after I took just a few drops of that "heart healthy" herb when my heart stopped and I was headed for Heaven.

∞ ∞ ∞

As I ponder those days just before I died, I now believe that my heart was breaking little-by-little. I was living with an "achy-breaky" heart in the midst of an "achy-breaky" world. Since none of the usual causes of heart disease were in my life, except for stress, it was only logical to assume that the cause of my death had not been from physically harmful abuse of my body, but from emotional pain my heart could not bear. My heart did not fail due to the virus or the injection, but because of the emotional turmoil of the covid world which had a devastating, detrimental effect on all who went through it and survived.

Obviously, my heart was more beaten and battered by all the stress of those covid years than I realized. I came to the painful reality that my heart had been burdened with the pain of too much of that which was too much. My heart had been damaged not only because of all I was going through emotionally regarding my own concerns, but also for all my family, friends, strangers, America, and the world.

Before the years of covid, I was thankful and happy to have survived and thrived after having endured more of a takotsubo life than I would have preferred. I was in my 60s, looking and feeling better than most my age. A lifetime of faith in the Lord in the midst of unbelievable and frequent tribulations had sustained me so much that I felt as if all that didn't kill me sure must have made me so strong that I was "spiritually inoculated" from any further damage from the woes of this world. This included whatever stress that would unfold in our "covid world." I was also beginning to feel that I had already done all I was supposed to have done with my life. I thought that just as I had outlived my Delta® pension, I had outlived my purpose. I had loved and served God, my family, and had given my best at every assignment in life. My heart had been strong to help those I love, but was not strong enough to help myself. More and more I was feeling as if I was no longer needed nor wanted, and did not have the strength nor resources to even keep trying. But my value was not based on how I felt, but in how God felt about me: *"Jesus loves me, this I know, for the Bible tells me so*...God has been with me since He formed me in my mother's womb, and He will not leave me now:

"My health may fail, and my spirit may grow weak, but God remains the strength of my heart; he is mine forever" (Psalm 73:26, NLT).

"I made you, and I will care for you. I will carry you along and save you"
(Isaiah 46:1, NLT).

Chapter 16

DON'T DIE BEFORE YOU'RE DEAD

*"The thief's purpose is to steal and kill and destroy. My purpose is to give **... a rich and satisfying life**"* (John 10:10 NLT, emphasis added).

*"... I have set before you life and death, blessings and curses. **Now choose life**....so that you and your children may live"* (Deuteronomy 30:19 NIV, emphasis added).

*"But the godly shall flourish like palm trees and grow tall as the cedars of Lebanon. For they are transplanted into the Lord's own garden and are under his personal care. **Even in old age they will still produce fruit and be vital and green**. This honors the Lord and exhibits his faithful care. He is my shelter. There is nothing but goodness in him!"* (Psalm 92:12-15, emphasis added).

*"Teach us to number our days and recognize how few they are; help us to spend them as we should. O Jehovah, come and bless us! .... Satisfy us in our earliest youth with your loving-kindness, **giving us constant joy to the end of our lives**. Give us gladness in proportion to our former misery! Replace the evil years with good. Let us see your miracles again; let our children see glorious things....and let the Lord our God favor us and give us success. May he give permanence to all we do"*
(Psalm 90:12-17, emphasis added).

*"**He has made everything beautiful in its time**. He has also set eternity in the human heart; yet no one can fathom what God has done from beginning to end"*
(Ecclesiastes 3:11 NIV, emphasis added).

On earth, given enough time, everything crumbles, nobody remembers us and, eventually, the only response at any mention of our name will be, "Who were they?" We devote all our time to be known, and yet we will one day be forgotten. Life is ultimately meaningless and absurd if you don't understand what God has given you in His Word to give meaning to this life, and it's difficult to make it all the way through life without it.

Only in Jesus Christ is it possible for us to discover the meaning of life and the eternal purpose of our lives.

Ecclesiastes 3:11 tells us that God has put eternity into our hearts. This means that every single human has a hunger and longing for God, even if we do not know it. There is an empty place in one's heart that only God can fill.

In our culture, we try to fill that void with everything in *this* world to find meaning and satisfaction in life: relationships, money, sex, drugs, ambition, pride, sports, entertainment, houses, food, travel, popularity, parties, power, but everything we stuff into the empty spaces of our hearts does not fit. As King Solomon wisely concluded in Ecclesiastes 1:2, King James Version (KJV): *"Vanity of vanities, all is vanity."*

The New Living Translation (NLT) expounds upon wise King Solomon's words:

> *"Everything is meaningless....completely meaningless!"*
>
> *"What do people get for all their hard work under the sun? Generations come and generations go, but the earth never changes. The sun rises and the sun sets, then hurries around to rise again. The wind blows south, and then turns north. Around and around it goes, blowing in circles. Rivers run into the sea, but the sea is never full. Then the water returns again to the rivers and flows out again to the sea. Everything is wearisome beyond description. No matter how much we see, we are never satisfied. No matter how much we hear, we are not content.*
>
> *History merely repeats itself. It has all been done before. Nothing under the sun is truly new. Sometimes people say, "Here is something new!" But actually it is old; nothing is ever truly new."*

Nothing can fit in the space of our heart that is meant to be filled with what matters most. There will always be something missing without God.

When missionaries traveled to Papua, New Guinea for the first time, they were surprised to find people there who had a hunger for the God they did not know. They made idols, built shrines, and devised rituals in hope of filling the void in their hearts, but all in futile attempts to find, know and worship the God their hearts yearned for. No matter how many gods they conjured up, there was need for more. When told about Jesus and the one true God, they knew they had found what they were looking for. In cultures throughout the world, both the "uncivilized" as well as those in "civilized" societies, people seek to know the one and only God to fill the emptiness in their hearts. We were not built for this world; we were built for eternity. Until we find real purpose to fill the void in our lives, we will never have the wonderful feeling that "all is well." Only Jesus can give us meaning that will satisfy that longing in our hearts.

Nothing, absolutely nothing, in this world is ever enough. You would think that at least those who reach the pinnacle of success would be totally satisfied, but it "ain't so."

One example of this is to learn about those who have spent their entire lives dreaming and working towards winning the Super Bowl and placing on their fingers a coveted Super Bowl ring. However, studies show that after about 15 years, most Super Bowl Championship rings held no value for the recipients; they were gone – either sold, donated, or pawned. Even a championship victory and seemingly priceless ring could not fill the void in the hearts of the most ambitious and talented football players.

Decades ago, I enjoyed watching a woman tennis professional compete. I don't remember anything about her matches or life other than what she said during an interview after winning the US Open tennis championship. When asked about her amazing accomplishment, she mentioned how the night after winning, she was alone in her plush hotel suite and was overcome with the feeling of, "That's it?" She, too, had worked diligently all her life toward a goal that she thought meant everything to her, but ultimately it meant nothing.

Steve Jobs enjoyed a lifestyle as one of the world's richest men, but it wasn't until he was dying that he realized he had never truly lived. Shortly before he died, he wrote of the delusion of his life: "In the end, my wealth is only a fact of life that I am accustomed to. At this moment, lying on my bed and recalling my life, I realize that all the recognition and wealth that I took so much pride in, have paled, and become meaningless in the face of my death."

The pleasures of this temporary world just cannot compare to the treasures of eternity:

> *"...no mere man has ever seen, heard, or even imagined what wonderful things God has ready for those who love the Lord."* (I Corinthians 2:9).

St. Augustine sums it up best in his notable prayer: "You have made us for yourselves, and our hearts are restless until they learn to rest in Thee."

When someone dies, written on their tombstones along with the day they were born, are often the words "...entered into eternal rest on such and such a date" — or "entered into eternal life...." Our "eternal rest" and "eternal life" are not when we meet in the "sweet by and by." Our eternal rest and eternal life begin when we receive Jesus Christ as our Savior. You are never to be able to "rest" in the satisfaction of life and begin eternal life until Jesus fills the vacuum in your heart. When we die, it merely is a step forward into eternal life as God had originally created all of life to be. Jesus lives in us through the presence of the Holy Spirit who enlarges our purpose to live until we die; love how we live; not die before we are dead!

It seems like we are living in a world with no one in charge, but when Jesus fills the void in our hearts, we do have "joy, joy, joy in [our] hearts to stay" with assurance that "He has the whole world in His hands."

But our lives are to be more than just existing from one day to the next. When you are a child of God, you are to live a richly rewarding and even a fun life as a "spiritual avenger" capable of supernaturally infused talents and skills to be victorious in every daily assignment. We are fearfully and wonderfully made with exponentially more value than just to be able to pile up "treasures" in this world and leave them all behind.

We are reminded multiple times in the Scriptures of how short our lives are:

"For we were born but yesterday and know nothing. Our days on earth are as fleeting as a shadow" (Job 8:9, NLT).

"Lord, help me to realize how brief my time on earth will be. Help me to know that I am here for but a moment more. My life is no longer than my hand! My whole lifetime is but a moment to you. Proud man! Frail as breath! A shadow! And all his busy rushing ends in nothing. He heaps up riches for someone else to spend" (Psalm 39:4-5).

God gives us richly all things in this world to enjoy, but it is not the things of this world that make life most enjoyable, rewarding and fulfilling. What we do with the things He gives us determines our joy and destiny. To not die before we are dead exists in knowing and experiencing the presence and power of God, and to use all we've been given in this temporary world for what matters most from an eternal perspective.

"Command those who are rich in this present world not to be arrogant nor to put their hope in wealth, which is so uncertain, but to put their hope in God, who richly provides us with everything for our enjoyment. Command them to do good, to be rich in good deeds,

and to be generous and willing to share. In this way they will lay up treasure for themselves as a firm foundation for the coming age, so that they may take hold of the life that is truly life" (I Timothy 6:17-19, NIV).

If we live solely for this world, we will never be satisfied. If we do not understand our purpose, we will surrender to the burdens and anxieties of this world and merely exist with a void in our hearts.

The pleasures of this temporary world simply cannot compare to the treasures of eternity:

"...no mere man has ever seen, heard, or even imagined what wonderful things God has ready for those who love the Lord" (I Corinthians 2:9).

Even as men and women of faith, we can be overcome by the struggles in this world, so much so we will gradually let into our hearts damaging thoughts and concerns that replace our faith with fear. We can be tempted to give up or just get by with a lifeless and joyless existence from day to day. Sometimes if there's too much happening that just doesn't make sense, we will choose to look at the hopelessness we do see in the temporary, instead of trusting the reality of what we do not yet fully see in the eternal. Anytime we try to push out of our hearts "a little" of Jesus and try to push in the concerns of this world, we can lose sight of what matters most and what doesn't really matter at all.

Sometimes we do this by falling into a trap of living to get more of what we already have. We get irritated and annoyed so much at small stuff that we can't effectively handle the big stuff. Sometimes we just don't even want to think about what happens after we die, so we are tempted to merely exist day-to-day, doing whatever we please as if we will not die.

To live before we die means that we love more, forgive faster, and cherish the beauty within each day; we are kinder and laugh more; we value people over things; we discover what God created us for and work to be and become the best at it; we cherish heart connections rather than isolation, and we keep moving forward even through failure.

To choose life and not to die before you're dead means you cultivate the power within your heart to choose joy. What does this mean?

1. To recognize pain in this world is real, but we are not overcome by it: *"... in Me you may have peace. In the world you will have tribulation; but be of good cheer, I have overcome the world"* (John 16:33, NKJV).

2. Embracing the joy of Jesus in and through all things: *"...Don't be dejected and sad, for the joy of the Lord is your strength!"* (Nehemiah 8:10, NLT).

3. Meditate and focus on good things; to see the best even in the midst of bad things: *"Fix your thoughts on what is true and good and right. Think about things that are pure and lovely, and dwell on the fine, good things in others. Think about all you can praise God for and be glad about"* (Philippians 4:8).

4. Draw upon the power of God within you when you feel powerless: *"My grace is all you need. My power works best in weakness. So now I am glad to boast about my weaknesses, so that the power of Christ can work through me. That's why I take pleasure in my weaknesses, and in the insults, hardships, persecutions, and troubles that I suffer for Christ. For when I am weak, then I am strong"* (II Corinthians 12:9-10, NLT).

5. Look at life through our Father's eyes: *"The Lord doesn't see things the way you see them. People judge by outward appearance, but the Lord looks at the heart"* (I Samuel 16:7, NLT).

6. Understand that you are a high value target (HVT) in the Kingdom of God, but also you are covered by the blood of Jesus' protection, for darkness cannot survive in light: *"no weapon turned against you shall succeed"* (Isaiah 54:17).

7. You choose to not give up; instead, you choose to see potential for *shalom* in your life and the lives of those whom you love; you choose to trust God to realize the seven-fold meaning of shalom:

    1) *complete well-being* (Genesis 43:27); 2) *good health* (Genesis 43:28); 3 *safety* (I Samuel 18:20); 4) *favor* (Song of Solomon 8:10); 5) *tranquility* (Psalm 38:3); 6) *prosperity* (Psalm 35:27), and 7) *wholeness* (Deuteronomy 27:7).

It is never easy to do what is best. The determination to "not die before I am dead" is a focus I must daily fight for.

I would love to declare that after the extraordinary blessing of personally experiencing a phenomenal miracle, life is now all "sunshine and lollipops, peaches and cream." After all, I had won the fight of faith for life over death. So now life was going to be better than ever, right? Why can't life on earth now be for me like "chocolate and roses" until the Rapture?

While I had enjoyed a "honeymoon period" of seeing deeper dimensions of living, improved relationships and appreciation of everything, the realization was quite evident that my soul had reentered an imperfect body susceptible to all the sin and temptations as before I died. The fallen world had not changed during the brief time my soul was not in it. Although I was blessed with a Heaven-sent miracle, I was still to live in a world where hell was never ceasing to kill, steal, and destroy, and where I was still susceptible to all attacks of the enemy and needed to always be ready for battle.

In many ways, my life after I died became worse. Before I died, I was just another "ordinary" old and financially challenged widow struggling to make the rest of my life the best of my life; I was not much of a target for "fiery darts" of the enemy. I was so insignificant that I had been portrayed to millions of people as the worst of the worst cooks in America!

After I died and came to life again, I became a "walking miracle star" with a potential to shine a bright light in the dark plans of the enemy. Nobody but God could get glory in what happened to me. So with higher potential to live an eternally significant and far more powerful life than ever before, I was to become an HVT, a high value target to the enemy. Since the miracle, the attacks have been unceasing to keep me from sharing all that God has done. God did not allow the enemy to take my life, so now I am an HVT to keep me from talking about it and hinder any attempt at living victoriously and/or influencing anyone to trust in God and not in this world. Most assuredly, I was an HVT in my desire to be a Holy Spirit-filled grandma to my mighty warrior men of God grandsons and any future grandchildren.

Since my miracle, it seems at times as if "all hell has broken lose" to ensure that I cannot and do not actually practice what I preach. Not only have I been through some more attempts to take my life again, but attacks upon my emotions, mind, family, computer, phone, car, income, electricity... you name it. But it still "ain't over" until God says so.

∞ ∞ ∞

A hurricane is coming!

Warnings were broadcast on all media outlets multiple times each day: "Prepare for a massive hurricane that will cover all of Florida. Projections are for a direct impact on Jacksonville!"

It was just five months after I'd weathered the biggest storm of my life that fear of the "big one" threatened my peace. Water and other essentials were gone from grocery store shelves where anxious families made necessary preparations. Cars formed long lines at gas stations.

Phone alerts were frequent: "Take shelter; verify evacuation zones; hurricane warning for Duval County."

I'd lived in Florida long enough to know that the forecasts are wrong far more often than they are right. The "projected" paths looked to me like 1st graders were given a box of crayons to draw lines all over Florida based on what they thought would be the path of the hurricane.

But the warnings were enough in my weakened emotional state of mind to create an ominous feeling of doom.

Each of those days I cried out: "Oh Lord, You're already giving me another crisis I must deal with alone in this world. I am not ready for this!" It had only been months since my miracle, yet already I was doubting God's plans and purposes for my life.

Could meteorologists actually be right this time?

The perpetual and prolonged warnings made me wonder if there was a real possibility of impact near where I lived. After months of struggling quietly with concerning chest pain and heart palpitations, I was physically and emotionally too weak to overcome my anxiety.

I had been so very confident that I was spiritually strong enough to deal with everything, but now I was doubting I could handle anything.

Living through regular tornado warnings when dwelling alone in my Texas home reassured me of God's protection. One particular time, as sirens blared throughout my neighborhood and warnings on TV and cell phones were to take immediate shelter, I got into a closet with Happy and prayed for angel's wings to cover our house and neighborhood. When it passed, I learned that

172

a tornado did considerable damage at each end of my street and adjacent neighborhood, but not to any structures in my immediate neighborhood. I cannot remember ever being fearful in a storm except when I was at church camp once as a young teenager and we were camping on a mountain top with intense thunder and lightning surrounding us. I recall singing over and over the old hymn, *God Will Take Care of You©* (Fanny Crosby, 1820-1915) to calm my fears. More than 55 years later, a mere "hurricane warning" was making me feel like a frightened kid again. In Florida, I enjoyed other hurricane "crises" when evacuating with Gavin, Carson, Rachel, and Melody to a place where we enjoyed playing games, eating junk food and watching movies together. So I was surprised that this hurricane warning was making me feel so different. I took too much to heart the doom and gloom warnings, and my heart was just not as physically strong as before; fear was replacing faith in my heart. Also, my heart was even more weakened as I was still trying to recover from the loss of Karly. It would be the first hurricane warning without Karly or Happy with me.

Karly didn't handle any storm well. She needed constant attention and special care, but in giving her comfort she comforted me. Even though she would be so nervous and anxious, she would lay on my head, shaking, I still wanted and needed her with me and welcomed her "clingy" love. Our heart connection was mutually beneficial to diminish our mutual anxieties in the midst of howling winds and house-rattling thunder.

Karly had only been gone from this world for two months. I missed her more than words could express. My heart ached for her.

In August, a month after Karly was gone, I had been taking care of Archie at Melody's house while she was in NYC, and there was an intense storm. I held Archie close while looking out at the fierce winds and rain through the sliding glass doors at the back of her home.

"That sure looks like a tornado," I said calmly to Archie, a moment before we were startled by the piercing phone alarm: "Tornado warning. Take shelter." What Archie and I were witnessing did not just look like a tornado, it was a tornado strong enough to topple the large oak tree behind Melody's house and drop it onto a normally busy road where, thankfully, there had not been any cars. I took a screen shot of the radar map at the time of the tornado and was amazed to see the spot of the tornado we were in was in the shape of a heart. It was as if God had covered us with His protective love.

The heart connection I shared with Archie was so comforting that neither of us had even a moment of fear or anxiety when I held him in my arms. Holding Archie made me feel as if God was holding us both.

But this "new" storm, considered a hurricane, was more stressful than any other; the warnings were not just for a few hours, but went on for days. It was a "creeper" storm, apparently stalled over all of Florida. Day after day there were not just watches, but warnings of impending doom. It was hard to "think on good things" when constantly bombarded with the bad.

When the outer bands of the storm finally reached the Jacksonville area, I was driving on a bridge as waves of strong winds and rain pelted my car. I was nervously dodging debris and praying my car would not fly away.

The anxiety of possibly becoming trapped in the monster storm was causing me to have increased heart palpitations, and dull aching and shooting pains in the center of my chest.

"Please God, not another heart attack! No!"

I considered redirecting my "flying car" to the hospital, but instead took deep breaths to alleviate my chest pains, dizziness, and weakness; I trusted that I was merely having a panic attack, not a heart attack. At one point, I was so exasperated from being alone in the midst of it all that I walked out into the storm in the rain and wind and declared, "I don't care if I live or die."

The path of the worst intensity of the hurricane did not impact Jacksonville as forecast for days. I did lose electricity and internet and my car was covered with tree branches. The wind howled incessantly outside all night and rainwater seeped through the openings of the windows where seals had broken during prior hurricanes.

With only candlelight, I was to learn more of the meaning of *"rest in the Lord"* (Psalm 37:7).

I was convicted over my anxiety and reminded that fear cannot survive in a heart of faith.

"My health may fail, and my spirit may grow weak, but God remains the strength of my heart…" (Psalm 73:26, NLT). *"Fear not, for I am with you"* (Isaiah 41:10).

As faith replaced the fear in my heart, I was at peace as candlelight flickered while the winds were howling, the windows shaking, and tree leaves and limbs were flying past my windows. I kept the curtains open so I would know what was actually happening. Surrounding myself with comfy pillows on the couch, I began singing confessions of faith:

"I can do all things, through Christ who makes me strong…In my weakness, He is there to let me know….His strength is perfect, when our strength is gone…He'll carry us when we can't carry on…raised in His power, the weak become strong….

His strength begins when ours comes to an end…"

"Come to me, all you who are weary and burdened, and I will give you rest. Take my yoke upon you and learn from me, for I am gentle and humble in heart, and you will find rest for your souls. For my yoke is easy and my burden is light" (Matthew 11:28-30, NIV).

∞ ∞ ∞

After the "hurricane meltdown" I knew that even though I didn't consider my reclusive life and low status on the socioeconomic ladder of success to be a threat to the enemy, it made me aware that just as evil had tried to take the lives of all my family numerous times, every born again believer and follower of Jesus Christ is a potential threat and therefore is a target of evil:

"Yes, and everyone who wants to live a godly life in Christ Jesus will suffer persecution"
(II Timothy 3:12, NLT).

While all true Christians are targeted, if you are a significant threat or have great potential (such as young children who love God and those with considerable talents and abilities), then you will become a high value target (HVT). The greater the level of your mission, your calling, your purpose, and your potential, the greater your attacks as an HVT.

Jesus is the prime example of an HVT. From earliest human history, evil tried to prevent Him from entering into this world to save us and make a way for eternal life. The god of this world, satan, and all the most powerful entities of hell tried to prevent His birth, kill Him as a child, and tempt Him in the wilderness to prevent His sacrifice on the cross for forgiveness of our sins.

The term HVT was given to Osama Bin Laden who orchestrated the attacks on the United States on 9-11-2001. All the most elite and talented forces were trained to perfect their skills and energies upon him because he had the greatest influence to destroy us. In the military, resources are not wasted on those with little or no influence, only those who can do the ultimate damage.

As spiritual HVTs, we are targeted by high levels of principalities and powers who work through people, circumstances, and even through crashing computers, malfunctioning cars, disrupted phone service, sickness, family, finances, acquaintances, and strangers to do everything possible to stop us from our success and victory. The enemy cannot have what he wants most – our souls. Therefore, he incessantly attacks us and all things around us to try to discourage us, weaken us, and exhaust us physically, mentally, emotionally, and spiritually so we cannot become all that God created us for. If we are not equipped with the armor of God all the time, we will sometimes fail.

"For we are not fighting against people made of flesh and blood, but against persons without bodies—the evil rulers of the unseen world, those mighty satanic beings and great evil princes of darkness who rule this world; and against huge numbers of wicked spirits in the spirit world" (Ephesians 6:12).

It is the elite of demonic forces that attack spiritual HVTs. They may not be permitted to take our lives, but they can be effective in extinguishing the light of our lives. As Christians we are referred to as the "light of the world." Darkness cannot survive when there is light. A spiritual HVT is like a powerful spotlight that exposes and destroys darkness on a massive scale. A spiritual HVT reminds me of being much like a "direct energy weapon" against the kingdom of darkness from which our enemy has no chance to survive.

Ever wonder why some of the most terrible, unpleasant, dangerous people seem to have no problems and are able to sail through life getting pretty much whatever they want with adulation and unlimited resources? You can be sure they rarely encounter problems or tribulations because they are no threat to the evil which seeks to destroy all that God has created. The simple answer to the age-old question about why bad things happen to good people is that they are spiritual HVTs. That is why we must always be conscious of our need to put on our spiritual armor each day as instructed in God's Word:

"Be strong in the Lord and in his mighty power. Put on all of God's armor so that you will be able to stand firm against all strategies of the devil. For we are not fighting against flesh-and-blood enemies, but against evil rulers and authorities of the unseen world, against mighty powers in this dark world, and against evil spirits in the heavenly places"
(Ephesians 6:11-12).

We will be attacked. The higher your level of assignment, the greater will be your attacks. I would have preferred, when coming back to life on earth, for my days to be like "sunshine, lollipops and everything that's wonderful." I would be happy to encourage others with my miracle testimony, if asked about it. However, I would have been perfectly satisfied devoting my life to being the best grandma and grand-doggy mom possible. I consider investing, time, energy, and talent to help my grandsons as the most important work and ministry for me in my senior years. Therefore, I have had no desire to be a major "influencer" in an expanded way in this world. Yet, the very fact that I am breathing, walking, talking, and singing at all is a testimony of God's magnificent power and greatness; that in itself is a miracle that would make me an "influencer" whether I wanted to be or not. Consequently, some days would be as "burnt toast, blizzards and everything that's horrible."

It's not surprising that since I came back to life nearly every day has been more difficult. I don't want to magnify the work of the enemy, so I'm not going to write about all that has happened. We are not meant to dwell on evil, but to magnify good. We are not to focus on our weaknesses, but to realize God's strength. We are not to take on the cares of our own lives, our families, or the world, but to give it all to Jesus. The sooner we joyfully cast our cares to Jesus in and through our struggles, the sooner we can realize that no weapon formed against us will prosper. I can speak from over a half century of intense life experiences that in the midst of attacks we truly *can* be at peace in knowing "God's got this!"

"The Lord says, 'Don't be afraid! Don't be paralyzed by this mighty army! For the battle is not yours, but God's! (II Chronicles 20:15).

We learn from Bible HVTs that at times they too were discouraged, downtrodden, depressed, and weary in the battles. We are not to condemn those in the family of God who sometimes are not as positive as we expect a strong Christian to be. That is why we must cultivate close relationships with Spirit-filled family and friends so that we can support each other during seasons of attacks and help each other through all the "stuff" of living in this world.

Some examples of Bible HVTs who experienced discouragement and depression are:

1. Solomon: He was an HVT because he was the richest man in the world and was also given great wisdom from God, but his wisdom and riches made him a HVT with constant attacks to prevent him from being all God created him to be. His faith was attacked through

his weakness for foreign and godless women and thinking that "just one more" woman was needed instead of a perfect union with the one God desired for him. He also surrendered to the lie of believing excessive wealth was the source of satisfaction and contentment in life. Solomon was constantly attacked with the temptations of dismissing the satisfying wisdom of God and choosing the fake and empty wisdom of the world. Consequently, even though he had conquered every mortal enemy and possessed every material pleasure the world afforded, he so despaired of life that it had no real meaning for him. At least 24 times in Ecclesiastes, Solomon talked of the "vanity of vanities" of living life apart from God. Without God, life is empty, holds no real meaning, and provides no lasting significance.

2. Elijah: He was described as a "mighty warrior man of God." One of his greatest successes was when defeating 450 prophets of Baal. But an HVT is not just attacked during battles, but often even more after great victories. We assume that after our greatest success in this world, we will have it easy and the enemy will leave us alone. But attacks on this warrior HVT were so intense after his greatest triumph, that he prayed he "might die!"

3. Job: Wealthy and influential worshiper and servant of God, he was an HVT target of the highest degree. Like Solomon, Job was not immune to HVT attacks and was so depressed because of the battles that he wished he had never been born.

4. Jonah: As an HVT who, after was delivered from death in the stinky belly of a whale, later wanted to die.

5. Paul: Paul was living a comfortable and prestigious life when he was a God-hating man named Saul who killed Christians. It was only when he was transformed into the highest level HVT that his troubles were worse than most of us could ever conceive of or even survive, including: frequent imprisonment, snake bites, shipwrecks, and being stoned and left for dead. But Paul didn't give up and go to Heaven because life was just too "hard." In the midst of the battles he continued to share that Jesus Christ is the Messiah, while encouraging other spiritual HVTs to know a supremely satisfying life on earth of peace, joy and victory, and to finish the fight of faith before dying. The inspirational messages of his HVT life continues

to bless modern day HVTs through the 13 books he authored that are included in the New Testament. As the highest level HVT, he endured attacks that make our battles seem so very small. Paul understood the battle for life in this world is constant and great, but as we hope in God, our power is and will always be greater than any HVT attack: *"We do not want you to be uninformed, brothers and sisters, about the troubles we experienced in the province of Asia. We were under great pressure, far beyond our ability to endure, so that we despaired of life itself. Indeed, we felt we had received the sentence of death. But this happened that we might not rely on ourselves but on God, who raises the dead. He has delivered us from such a deadly peril, and he will deliver us again. On him we have set our hope that he will continue to deliver us."* (II Corinthians 1:8-10). Paul knew an HVT was to keep fighting, to never give up, to run the race, to finish the course: *"I am going to keep on being glad, for I know that as you pray for me, and as the Holy Spirit helps me, this is all going to turn out for my good. For I live in eager expectation and hope that I will never do anything that will cause me to be ashamed of myself but that I will always be ready to speak out boldly for Christ while I am going through all these trials here, just as I have in the past; and that I will always be an honor to Christ, whether I live or whether I must die. For to me, living means opportunities for Christ, and dying—well, that's better yet! But if living will give me more opportunities to win people to Christ, then I really don't know which is better, to live or die! Sometimes I want to live, and at other times I don't, for I long to go and be with Christ. How much happier for me than being here! But the fact is that I can be of more help to you by staying! Yes, I am still needed down here, and so I feel certain I will be staying on earth a little longer, to help you grow and become happy in your faith; my staying will make you glad and give you reason to glorify Christ Jesus for keeping me safe when I return to visit you again"* (Philippians 1:19-26). Paul reminds us more than anyone that no matter what we go through, nor how hopeless our situation, we can keep living a victorious, blessed, and beautiful life.

A modern-day highest level HVT is former President Donald Trump. While he does not have vast and notable Biblical knowledge, wisdom, and understanding, he professes in Jesus Christ as His Savior and has been willing to allow God to use him to fight and win battles which strengthen all Americans, especially those who know, love, and serve the Lord, to be and become the best we are created to be. Therefore, he is most hated by the

Kingdom of Darkness, as evidenced by how much and he and his family are relentlessly and perpetually attacked. What God inspires him to do can positively affect each of our personal lives, our nation, and the entire world – so he has been given the highest level of HVT assignments. God has revealed to us our part in the success of HVT leaders and HVTs with high levels of authority.

"I urge, then, first of all, that petitions, prayers, intercession and thanksgiving be made for all people — for kings and all those in authority, that we may live peaceful and quiet lives in all godliness and holiness" (I Timothy 2:1-2, NIV).

Praying for the highest level of those who are HVTs helps all of us to better overcome our positions of lower level HVTs.

In June of 2019, Daniel and I were seated on the first row across the aisle of VIP's including Governor DeSantis, several senators including Florida's Rick Scott, Marco Rubio, and notable religious leaders such as Jentzen Franklin, when Trump launched his 2020 reelection campaign at the massive Amway Center in Orlando, Florida. Our location put us in the televised images when Trump would mention any other HVT/ VIP. Every network and news outlet showed our profiles and smiles clearly visible in the bottom right corner of every television screen; it looked as if we were actually sitting alongside the VIPs. We didn't know it was happening until we both started seeing texts from people we knew who were watching. Out of the 20,000 people there, we were the only two "ordinary" people shown amongst the VIPs. I still laugh when thinking about it and sometimes still see online news outlets with photos in articles of that momentous day when Daniel and I sat next to VIPs. We were actually so close to President Trump that I think he heard me shout multiple times, "The best is yet to come," when he looked and pointed at what seemed to be my son and me. It was after that rally that Trump himself would often say, "The best is yet to come" throughout his campaign, so I naturally assumed I had inspired him to use that slogan. When recalling the day we were across the aisle from the VIP section of that event, I am reminded that although we may not seem to be a VIP in this world, we still can be an HVT-VIP through the mere commitment to faithfully pray for those in authority, for when we pray, Heaven responds.

Children who love God become HVTs not only because their faith is usually stronger than most adults, but also the potential for their influence is greater with a lifetime of possibilities to pierce and destroy the works of darkness.

Simply by having witnessed and been a part of my miracle, my grandsons are also HVTs. The enemy sure doesn't want them talking about what God has done. Just being young men who trust in the Lord is enough for them to be HVTs, but even more so since they have good and smart minds and hearts to do great things in this world which glorify God.

When they tell other kids about what happened to me, sometimes they are accused of lying, but it doesn't bother them; when we speak truth, we have peace. Since before they could talk, we were teaching them how to grow in wisdom, strength, and knowledge of the power of God, which encouraged them to each have a heart to know, love and serve Him. A few years ago at the beach, Carson spontaneously wrote in the sand, "I love God and I hate satan." This reflected the joy of the Lord in his heart and greatly blessed mine to see his desire to declare to the world the content of his heart. Recently Gavin has learned what happens as a mere 10-year-old HVT when he excels above other kids his age in tennis competitions where jealous kids he defeats, and even their parents, mock, ridicule and even curse at him with verbal attacks of false accusations. His strength, courage and skill have made him an HVT that others want to destroy. Being well aware of this, he designed a t-shirt to wear in competitions that has the image of a target and "HVT" on the front.

Both Gavin and Carson have learned about spiritual warfare since they were only 2 years old and wore "armor of God" costumes. These helped them know how important it is to put on the "armor of God" for protection and fortify their resolve that no weapon formed against them will prosper. They already understand that it is only those with the most potential for greatness that will be attacked the most.

As Gavin has always demonstrated a desire to grow in wisdom and knowledge of God's Word and purposes for his life and this world, he began reading the book of Revelation this past year. He has even had dreams of what might be happening in the future of our nation. The hearts of children are often more open to what God is and does, and I believe Gavin is one of those; so are Carson and Theodore. It is my heart's desire to encourage and support them to be and become all God created them to be. When I was Gavin's age, I was also drawn to read the book of Revelation, usually in church when the preacher's message was just not as interesting to me. My constant prayer is that my children and grandchildren will be far more victorious through the battles of life than I was, especially since it sure seems that much of what is written in Revelation seems to be happening in our lifetimes.

The "hurricane meltdown" was a reminder that what God did for me resulted in my growing into a spiritual HVT, whether I wanted to be or not. Just as the main artery of my physical heart had become clogged with cholesterol and had prevented me from sustaining physical life, my spiritual arteries had been clogged with the "cholesterol" of hopelessness, grief, strife, lack and "stinkin' thinkin'" that threatened my surrender to enemy forces and prevented living with joy, purpose, and light in this fallen world.

The inner sanctum of the heart of a believer is possessed by the Holy Spirit who is our Comforter. I would prefer to never get discouraged or tempted to give up and give in to the problems and pain of this world, but it is comforting to know that it is in my deepest moments of weakness when God reveals His love to carry me through. *"For we know how dearly God loves us, because he has given us the Holy Spirit to fill our hearts with his love"* (Romans 5: 5, NLT).

I know that the presence and power of my Lord and God who brought me back from death would not leave me without His victorious strength in life now as a spiritual HVT.

"I have told you all this so that you may have peace in me. Here on earth you will have many trials and sorrows. But take heart, because I have overcome the world"
(John 16:33, NLT).

"The righteous person may have many troubles, but the Lord delivers him from them all"
(Psalm 34:19, NIV).

".... the joy of the Lord is your strength. You must not be dejected and sad!"
(Nehemiah 8: 10).

"Because the Lord is my Shepherd, I have everything I need!
He lets me rest in the meadow grass and leads me beside the quiet streams. He gives me new strength. He helps me do what honors him the most.
Even when walking through the dark valley of death I will not be afraid, for you are close beside me, guarding, guiding all the way.
You provide delicious food for me in the presence of my enemies. You have welcomed me as your guest; blessings overflow! Your goodness and unfailing kindness shall be with me all of my life, and afterwards I will live with you forever in your home" (Psalm 23).

God not only restored my strength and reignited the joy in my heart, but He also clarified for me more about how to truly live before I died – again. As I trusted Him *one day at a time,* He would make a way when there seemed to be no way.

∞ ∞ ∞

"But God, I am old and have nothing," I complained to Him one day when heart palpitations and chest pain had lingered even after my renewed commitment to not die. I've been a struggling widow forever, was worn out from working so much for so little, and had devoted my life to fight for my children, bless my family, and give my best even when I did not have the best. When I think of all the truly amazing people who did not survive sudden cardiac arrest – men and women with boundless resources on earth to truly give and live for a very long time, talented individuals blessed with endearing families, countless friends, and obviously influential socioeconomic status – I feel that they would have been so much better to have been resurrected. I did not understand the "What for?" He chose me to be one of the survivors. Perhaps it was to be a message of how God's love and care and eternally significant purpose is not just for those who "have it all." And to encourage anyone still alive and discouraged in this chaotic world, to know the desire of God is of unlimited potential for the rich, poor, old, young and everyone in between who trusts in Him. Gavin's declaration that "God is not finished with G-Joy yet," is obviously a reality that I must take to heart. And for me, being "old" is no reason to die...not yet.

Our human logic assumes the people who have the most in this world and have the most to lose when they leave it, should be the ones whose lives matter most. But our worth in the eternal Kingdom of God is not dependent on how much worth we have in this temporary kingdom of earth. Just in knowing that out of the billions ever born, no one shares the same fingerprints (except identical twins) is evidence of how God has uniquely given every person a unique destiny and purpose that is not to be ended before it is completed. He also gives us the choice to believe in Him or not; to trust in Him with all our hearts or not; to pray or not to pray for His will to be fulfilled in our individual lives, and to choose to live until we die or die before we're dead.

∞ ∞ ∞

When moving to Florida more than 10 years ago, one thing I noticed and loved most was that there were palm trees everywhere. Palm trees are beautiful, but also are created to survive the worst of storms and attempts to kill them. Palm trees remain strong no matter how fierce the winds and extremes of all sorts of weather and challenges of the Florida environment. They perpetually grow new, beautiful branches and not only survive but thrive, even bearing such nutritious delights as dates, coconuts, figs. acai, betel nuts, and peaches. Since so many in their older years are drawn to this "Palm Tree State," perhaps, like me, they need to be reminded of what God tells us about how He created us to remain strong in our purpose and flourish and bear fruit no matter how old we are.

"The righteous will flourish like a palm tree,
they will grow like a cedar of Lebanon; planted in the house of the Lord,
they will flourish in the courts of our God.
They will still bear fruit in old age,
they will stay fresh and green" (Psalm 92:12-14, NIV).

"But Lord, I just can't do things like I could before. How can I possibly do anything significant now?" I again argued with God during one of my middle-of-the-night moments after I was awakened by chest pains which I had been assured were "just" angina or pericarditis or muscular-skeletal or stress related. But with a still, small voice speaking to my heart, I was reminded of His written Word:

"I will be your God through all your lifetime, yes, even when your hair is white with age. I
made you and I will care for you. I will carry you along and be your Savior"
(Isaiah 46:4).

"My life is an example to many, because you have been my strength and protection.
That is why I can never stop praising you; I declare your glory all day long.
And now, in my old age, don't set me aside. Don't abandon me when my strength is
failing" (Psalm 71:7-12, NLT).

How could I argue with God?

Just four months after the miracle, I officiated a wedding and began to book new ones. My first model job was five months after the miracle, which I felt made God laugh, for I was hired to act as a hospital patient! I'd sure had plenty of experience that year to prepare for that job.

The next job after I had died and returned was better than any job I had ever worked, not just as a model but as anything. Again, I felt that my job caused God to laugh because of who I was working for. God promised me I would "bear fruit in old age" and I was now working for the best fruit product of all with the Florida orange juice business. What's more, I was booked along with my daughter Melody Joy, who had saved my life. She has been a successful model for years, and it has always been my heart's desire to work with her in a commercial (or a movie). Once we were both offered roles for a commercial filmed in Tampa, but she was unavailable.

The client for Florida orange juice wanted a real life mom and daughter for their commercial, and the producer told us later that he just knew we would be the best. All the years I had been praying for the Holy Spirit to move upon the hearts of producers, clients, and agents to feel led to choose Melody and me for the same commercial finally had happened. But as a "fruit bearing senior" it would magnify my status as an HVT, and I was attacked the night before the shoot with chest pains that kept me awake and motivated Melody to research online for the closest emergency hospital "just in case." That "fiery dart" weapon formed against me did not prosper. We had the most beautiful and wonderful experience at Anna Maria Island, Florida filming for the Florida Orange Juice Association. An added blessing was through my model granddaughter with whom Melody had been a "model mom" before. Her name is Faith. So this shoot had a Grandma Joy, Daughter Melody and Granddaughter Faith. Wow, now that is what I call a "God-thing!" Our "family" trio was a reminder of how the rest of my days would be the best of my days. God's "song of joy" over my life was symbolized through this commercial with my real life and model daughter Melody Joy. My desire to sustain the joy of the Lord in my heart through faith was symbolized by a joy-filled model granddaughter named Faith. God's plan for me to have a "fruitful" old age was symbolized in how the best job I ever had was as representative of oranges, my favorite fruit.

In my condo I have a large drawing of Jesus laughing and have handed out wallet-sized cards with this image for more than 20 years. My "Melody Joy-Faith-and-fruit" job reminded me how I think Jesus had to have laughed throughout that fun commercial shoot.

On my first "birthday" of April 23, 2023, I wanted to celebrate big, but at least enjoyed a small celebratory remembrance and wrote letters of appreciation to those who had blessed me in the hospital the year before. My friend Claire had taken me to celebratory lunches at least once a month since the miracle, so I had already been perpetuating celebrating life for the entire year.

My first birthday (in 1955) was when I was born into the earth; my second was in 1960 when my spirit was born again into the Kingdom of God. After my third birthday in 2022 when my soul was returned to my earth body, some things were better, but some things were worse. The good things were so good that they helped balance out the worst.

Just after my one year "3rd birthday," I awoke one morning with both arms in pain and "frozen." I could barely move to get up. It was the strangest phenomenon, and one with which I was totally unfamiliar. Since I had watched thousands of hours of cardiologists and other doctors online and learned how to best heal my heart, I spent days researching what to do about my arms, but nothing I learned to do, no supplement I took, made any difference. When I began to get more chest pains in addition to two frozen shoulders, I knew I couldn't delay in getting medical help and went to the emergency room at the familiar Baptist Beaches Medical Center in Jacksonville.

Based on my symptoms it was *assumed* I had indeed had another heart attack. They gave me nitroglycerin to immediately dissipate the chest pains, but the arm pain intensified. Surprisingly, the tests revealed that I had *not* had a heart attack. Although I still had some issues that needed attention to overcome (including painfully frozen arms), I believe the main purpose of having gone to the hospital was to confirm that the MHM therapy God had instilled in my heart to pursue had worked. Doctors were amazed at what they discovered about my heart through their extensive tests.

After a year of prayerfully engaging in unconventional MHM cardiac therapy, music therapy, joy therapy, heart health research, and primarily consuming only heart building foods and supplements, it became apparent that the "hopeless" diagnosis for my future was not God's ordained destiny for me.

On May 2, 2023, my heart had become twice as strong. Part of my heart was still considered dead, but the heart that was not dead was keeping my total heart alive. Perhaps the chest pains I had been dealing with were only growing pains, as I had been growing a new heart. After "the widow-maker," my ejection fraction was about 30% with no expectation of it ever being more than 40%, which is still in the "heart failure" category, but God knew I need a much better functioning heart to truly live. It had increased to 62%, well within the "normal" category for healthy people between 50-70.

Praise God from whom all blessings flow! I was living proof of what God meant in Psalm 92:

"They will still bear fruit in old age, they will stay fresh and green,"

(Psalm 92:14, NIV).

I started to feel more "fresh and green" than ever!

Two days later, on my 68th birthday, Carson ran up to me on a tennis court and I joyfully hugged him back while picking him up off his feet. Yes, I was easily able to pick up Carson! He was super excited for me to open the gift he and Gavin had for my 68th birthday. Before I did, Melody showed up with the most beautiful flower bouquet I have ever seen, and Rachel followed behind with festive decorated cookies with lots of icing just like I have always enjoyed. Just the day itself was a gift from God with crystal clear, deep blue skies dotted with the fluffiest and whitest "cotton candy" clouds and a perfect 72 degrees. Carson was smiling mischievously as if he knew something I didn't. He was anxious for me to open my present. It was a box with the singing, "money, money, money…" while genuine dollar bills, 2 dollar bills, 5, 10, 20 dollar bills started to shoot up in the air and all over the tennis court. The box also said, "You've hit the jackpot!"

It was indeed a "jackpot day!" My 68th birthday continued with a visit to Epcot™ for the Flower and Garden Festival. It is my favorite and most beautiful time of year there; I can never get enough of flowers! We also enjoyed the amazing butterfly pavilion and shared a delightful lunch entertained by hibachi cooking. When Theo joined us it completed my joyful "Heaven on earth" celebration. With all my grandsons and flowers and "flying money," I was living one of those "fresh-and-green-in-old-age" days promised to the righteous in Psalm 92.

A couple weeks later, on Mother's Day, I auditioned with Gavin and Carson to work a commercial at Epcot™ in response to a nationwide casting call for real life grandmas and grandkids. Since hundreds would audition, we understood that there was a miniscule chance of being selected for such a fun job, but we enjoyed just trying.

Those who do not do this kind of work usually do not understand that you love it, even when you are rejected far more than selected for any role. The day we filmed the audition was fun, as Gavin and Carson are such talented "pros," having also done commercials before.

Two days later, I was informed that I had been selected for the role but was at first disappointed that confirmation did not include the boys. Just as I had been praying for more model jobs to work with Melody, I had also prayed since the HGTV™ shoot (in which we had such a phenomenally fun time with the participation of Gavin and Carson), that God would open doors for us to do commercials together. Well, it had finally happened. Fifteen minutes after confirming me as the "Epcot™ Grandma," Mark Mullen Casting called to confirm Gavin and Carson would join me. Hallelujah!

When Daniel was only one year old, and the twins just six weeks old, my Mom and Dad joined us for our first trip to Epcot™ that had opened the year Daniel was born. It had been the best day ever. Every year since, we have enjoyed inspirational family trips there, which can seem as if we were traveling throughout the world in just one day. My favorite time of year has always been the Flower and Garden Festival when shared with my children and grandsons. So, it didn't take much acting skills to show delight in being there when filming the commercial; it was our natural response to do so. Epcot™ is our favorite park. Our other favorite season there is at Christmas. Each day, a celebrity reads the scriptural account of the birth of Jesus between carols sung by a 200-voice choir holding candles. It always concludes with the *Hallelujah Chorus* and me crying tears of joy.

But on the day Gavin, Carson and I filmed the commercial at Epcot™ I wanted to sing the *Hallelujah Chorus* and cry. It was the best day ever! I never imagined after all those years of making cherished family memories going to Epcot™, that I would be with my two oldest grandsons being followed around by a film crew feeling like VIPs doing what we loved to do, what we were uniquely gifted to do, and getting paid to do it. I know that God was reminding me of His promise in Psalm 92 to make me "fresh and green" in my old age, because in both the Florida orange juice and Epcot™ commercials, the director had me wear green. I had been through some of the worst experiences since I died, but God gave me some of the best ever to balance them out.

Being an HVT, cardiac arrest surviving grandma meant that I would be attacked the night before the Epcot™ shoot the same way I had been the night before the Florida orange juice shoot. I couldn't sleep because of intense heart palpitations and pain that even all my usual healing music and heart supplements did not cure. Through persistent prayer, they subsided by our early 5:30AM departure to Orlando. I felt great all day, but had to figure out a way to cover up the dark circles under my eyes from no sleep and not look so sleep deprived when filming.

I have often quoted and declared the promises of God in Psalm 37:

> *"Delight yourself also in the Lord, And He shall give you the desires of your heart"*
> (Psalm 37:4, NKJV).

God does give us desires of our heart when we delight in Him, however, we do not always realize all the desires of our hearts. I don't understand why some desires are delayed while others are not. I was and am so very thankful that huge desires of my new heart were being realized in ways that were never known with my old heart.

In 2023, the first full year after I had died and survived, I was living the dream of having fulfilled some of the most fun and wonderful desires of my heart in commercials in the most heavenly beautiful places in this earthly world *and* with my daughter and grandsons who had been an important part of my miracle. I know those emotionally blessed "merry heart moments" truly *did* help physically heal my heart. Although between "Heaven on earth days," there have still been days filled with more earthly grief than I would prefer, I am energized and motivated to keep moving forward because of ever growing understanding of how God really *does* work all things together for good for those who love Him and are called according to His purposes. His purpose for me is the same for *all* those He loves, which is to live with joy, peace, satisfaction, and fulfillment until we die, trusting in Him to give us strength and favor to not let our dreams and mission die *before* we are dead, *before* the good work God began in us is complete.

Since God has been teaching me how to live "fresh and green" in my old age, I have composed a "Joy 777 list" with 777 ways to remind me of how to be and become all God created me for until my time on earth is complete. The number 7 is symbolic of perfection in the Bible, where it appears over 700 times. The number 7 is also associated with wisdom, intuition, growing self-awareness, spiritual revelations, and big changes that have a most positive impact on your life. It is also a number considered to serve as a bridge or connection between our mortal realm and higher places. In Biblical numerology, the number 7 is symbolic of completion and Divine wholeness.

Therefore, my list is to help me fulfill all the perfect purposes of God to complete the good work He began in me from the moment I was conceived.

I encourage you to write your own "777" list to reference as you continue to fulfill God's purposes for your life. To help you get started, consider 77 of what is on my personal 777 list:

DON'T DIE BEFORE YOU'RE DEAD/HEART OF JOY 777 CHECKLIST: First 77

1. Trust in the Lord through all of life the things you understand and the things you don't.

2. Choose joy in the midst of good times and even more so in the bad.

3. Don't sweat the small stuff.

4. Laugh more...A LOT more.

5. Enjoy Merry Heart Moments with people/pets/God every single day (even more if in the hospital or isolated some other way).

6. Sing when you're glad, sing when you're sad, and sing all the time in between.

7. Appreciate those closest to you; never take them for granted.

8. Get a happy dog and/or find a way to spend more time with animals.

9. Celebrate big moments big time.

10. Celebrate ordinary delights in extraordinarily ordinary ways.

11. Listen to inspirational and joyful music often.

12. Have fun doing what you love; make what you do not love fun.

13. Give thanks for and rejoice in those who can do what you cannot do and actually do it.

14. Find what you love to do and become the best at it.

15. Enjoy good, funny, interesting movies, programs, concerts, and athletic competitions.

16. Study Ephesians 6 in every Bible translation and version to learn how to put on the armor of God and live victoriously every day as a HVT.

17. Take walks in beautiful and inspirational places.

18. Read books that make you smile.

19. Watch the news enough to know what's going on in the world, but not too much to limit living in the world.

20. Eat food you love and that loves you; eat really good food really slowly.

21. Talk to God more than anyone else...even more than your dog.

22. Sometimes you need to eat ice cream, but only consume chemical-free delights.

23. Send a note through the mail to tell someone what you like most about them.

24. Think on good, good, good things.

25. Give the non-good thoughts to God.

26. Pray all the time about everything, everywhere.

27. Celebrate each birthday bigger than the birthday before.

28. If you feel like screaming, then you probably need to, but try to do so where only God can hear you.

29. When someone tells you to "be strong," realize that the joy of the Lord is your strength to be strong when your strength is all gone.

30. Seek to find work you live for and not just work to live.

31. Recognize when your cup is overflowing and to pour cups for others.

32. Don't argue with fools; don't even *think* about it.

33. Enjoy uninterrupted sleep on comfortable beds with down-filled pillows.

34. You will not always succeed, no matter how hard you try, so when you fail, fail *forward*.

35. Put the past, past; embrace the joys of the present and possibilities of the future.

36. Dancing is not just for professionals, so dance when the spirit moves you.

37. If you can't sleep, then pray and try singing.

38. To Be Blessed, Be a Blessing (TBBBAB).

39. Gaze at beautiful skies and discover how they will energize your soul.

40. If someone who hurts you walks away, move on, and as far away as you can.

41. Listen to your gut.

42. Do not gaze or meditate upon that which hurts your heart.

43. Discover the fun and joy in harmless peculiarities in people, animals, and all life.

44. Never say never to the blessings and opportunities of new things.

45. Read books that make you smile.

46. Keep trusting in God, no matter what people think, and even through "doomsday news."

47. Do not love money, love what God can do with money through you.

48. Learn to think; do not believe everything you hear.

49. Savor the unlimited flavors of the world.

50. Limit alcohol and expand horizons of satisfying fun without it.

51. Hug your children and your grandchildren with whom you share a heart connection no matter what their ages.

52. Stay away from "joy-stealers", people and things.

53. Never intentionally cause harm; immediately make right anything you unintentionally do wrong.

54. Take lots of pictures and take time to look at the pictures you take.

55. Embrace the hope in knowing the best is yet to come; there is life yet to live.

56. Ask God to show you the way when there seems to be no way and for the strength and resources to travel the right way.

57. Hug your pets and play with them multiple times every day.

58. Play at work and work at play.

59. Do more on earth than you wish you would have done when you get to Heaven.

60. Never think you are too young to do what you love and become the best at it.

61. Never consider yourself too old to do what you love to do.

62. Raise your children up in prayer no matter how much they might drag you down.

63. Realize in this world stuff happens, but your joy is not from stuff.

64. Cherish the benefits of rest as much as work and work as much as you rest.

65. You never lose what you give away.

66. Make sure your destiny is Heaven through a personal relationship with Jesus Christ as your Lord and Savior. Confess and repent of your sins; acknowledge the blood of Jesus forgives you; surrender your heart to the Lord, and become born again.

67. Pray with the assurance that God loves you, likes you, and has a wonderful plan for your life that no mere man can give or take away.

68. Support those who do good; do not waste your time and talents on those who do not.

69. Recognize those closest to you and most connected to your heart need your love and care, and you need theirs more than anyone else's in the world.

70. Consume into your soul and spirit at least one Bible verse of power, love, victory, and strength every day through music, prayer, and meditation.

71. Make what matters most, matter most, where it matters most.

72. Become angry only at that which is evil.

73. Surround yourself with good, good company and learn to know the difference.

74. Make yourself and your surroundings as colorful and beautiful as can be, especially with flowers.

75. Understand the meaning of *shalom* and ask the Holy Spirit to bless you and those you love with this every day.

76. Never give up, never give in; understand that you sometimes just won't understand, and give it all to Jesus.

77. LOVE, LOVE, LOVE; be faithful and loyal to those you love and who love you. Love God with all your heart, mind, body, and soul.

You are never too old to keep living, doing what you love to do, or at least trying. For me, it's doing what I'd wanted to do as a kid and I most enjoy now in my senior years: participating in a job which brings joy to others and is a joy to my heart. Officiating at weddings and celebratory events has been one such job, but acting and modeling at my age are especially fun. I get to enjoy being around some of the most creative, inspirational and artistic people in the world; every assignment is uniquely different than any other; I get to pretend to work at jobs I would have enjoyed in real life; I get to enjoy making the product or service I promote look extra good; I get to enjoy sometimes working with my family and feeling like those I work with are family; I actually get paid better than any other "normal" job in my life, and it helps me be "fresh and green" and fruitful in my senior years doing what I love to do and being the best at it.

When I saw Dolly Parton featured in a sparkly bodysuit and Dallas Cowboy cheerleaders' attire, singing her hit songs at a nationally televised NFL football game over Thanksgiving weekend in 2023, I thought, *now that is a woman who understands what it means to live until you die.* She was doing what she loves at age 77. Retirement is not in the Bible, and retirement is not for those desiring to be and become the best God created them to be. From what I know of Dolly's life, she has been a woman determined to live life to the fullest, no matter what anyone thinks; it only matters what is in her heart.

Another amazing 77-year-old is President Trump. His strong heart and determination to be and become all God created him to be are an inspiration. At an age when most retire to a life of endless ease and luxury, he is still working to bless an entire nation as he has been so greatly blessed. He understands that as a HVT, he must always be ready for battle and never give up, no matter how continuous and hurtful the attacks are.

Donald and Dolly are most certainly living proof of what it means in old age to "flourish like palm trees and bear fruit." But you might be thinking that it is easier for them to not "die until they're dead." To be sure, there are advantages to wealth and fame, but merely having wealth and fame is not the primary motivation, nor necessary for someone to live a richly rewarding life. If that were true, then why are all of the rich and famous not the happiest people on earth?

Nothing this world has to offer can give us satisfying joy and eternally rewarding purpose. It is only what God equips us with to live in this world that gives satisfying purpose. When we live knowing we matter to God, we are empowered to live a life that truly matters on earth-and in Heaven. With the joy of the Lord as our strength, we can knock down any of the "giants" that try to prevent our purpose and become giants ourselves.

We must move forward with enthusiasm for what God desires for us. The word "enthusiasm" originates from the Greek word, *enthous*, meaning "possessed, inspired by God." We have the energy of God in us. There is a surge of power that is like an "atomic reaction" in our hearts which can help us "barrel" forward into the remainder of God's Will for our lives. A fire to live burns in our hearts, not because of earthly comfort, but rooted in Divine courage to keep moving forward in the face of opposition, cultural change, and when confronted with the unknown future. God created our lives to count, not to merely be counted. Each day we must prayerfully step out of our "safe zone" into the faith zone. We are risk-takers, spiritual avengers who will stay exuberant about our lives and enthusiastic to be and become the best God has created us for.

No matter what season of life it is for you or for me, our brightest day is always around the corner as we let go of the past, always moving forward into whatever God has planned for the rest of our lives.

Just as a person is never too old to truly live a life of purpose and joy, one is never too young.

Not many years ago, we got to know of a beautiful young girl named Kate Amato who enjoyed shopping at the KYDS children's boutique my daughters own in Neptune Beach, Florida. Everyone who knew Kate loved her. She was the type of little girl whose sparkling smile would brighten any room and whose kind and loving spirit blessed all around her. In 2014, when just nine years old, she was diagnosed with a rare cancer that took her earthly life just over 2 years later. Although cancer took her out of this world, it could not take her life. Beautiful Kate truly lived every day with hope and desire to be a blessing of love, joy, beauty, and life as she had been so greatly blessed. Kate not only breathes the air of Heaven now and is living the best part of her eternal life, but her short time on earth is a gift that keeps on giving. The legacy of her amazing life continues to bless countless children and families battling cancer through the Kate Amato Foundation established in her honor. (https://kateamatofoundation.org/) A life that matters on earth, matters through all eternity.

I have a picture of Carson when he was about three years old taken at Epcot™ where he seems to be holding up "Spaceship Earth" with his tiny arms. I look at this photo often to remind me that God has the whole world in His hands and He does so through *tiny* us as we trust in *Him* with all our *hearts* for strength to do the *impossible*. Superimposed over this picture, I put words written by Kate Amato:

> Make the best of every day. Work hard, play hard, that's the way.
> Work hard to make it better and enjoy what you've done, make it
> for everyone.
> Swim in the flood...dance in the rain.
> Don't forget to smile.
> Shine through the pain.

Often it takes what is considered the "least" of life, such as the words of a little girl, to remind us of the best of life.

THE BEST IS YET TO COME!

ABOUT KHARIS PUBLISHING

Kharis Publishing, an imprint of Kharis Media LLC, is a leading Christian and inspirational book publisher based in Aurora, Chicago metropolitan area, Illinois. Kharis' dual mission is to give voice to under-represented writers (including women and first-time authors) and equip orphans in developing countries with literacy tools. That is why, for each book sold, the publisher channels some of the proceeds into providing books and computers for orphanages in developing countries so that these kids may learn to read, dream, and grow. For a limited time, Kharis Publishing is accepting unsolicited queries for nonfiction (Christian, self-help, memoirs, business, health, and wellness) from qualified leaders, professionals, pastors, and ministers. Learn more at: **https://kharispublishing.com/**

Milton Keynes UK
Ingram Content Group UK Ltd.
UKHW052304300624
444825UK00013B/387

9 781637 462485